THE
BALD
FACTS

THE
BALD
FACTS

THE DAVID ARMSTRONG
BIOGRAPHY

PAT SYMES
FOREWORD BY KEVIN KEEGAN

Pitch Publishing
A2 Yeoman Gate
Yeoman Way
Durrington
BN13 3QZ
www.pitchpublishing.co.uk

A CIP catalogue record is available for this book from the
British Library

ISBN-13: 978-1-90917-864-9

Typesetting and origination by Pitch Publishing.
Printed and bound by CPI Group (UK) Ltd, Croydon, CR0 4YY

Contents

Foreword

WHEN DAVID ARMSTRONG joined us at Southampton from Middlesbrough the players wanted to
see his birth certificate because we could not believe
someone who looked like him and had played 350 or so matches
could only be 26. We reckoned they must have doctored it in
the North-East and knocked ten years off his real age. David
seemed even then to have been around forever. I was pleased
Lawrie McMenemy had signed him for us because he had
always been an excellent player for Middlesbrough; capable,
tidy, he never gave the ball away and always had a good football
brain. Even when he was a youngster, coming into the team at
Middlesbrough, there was a maturity about him, a calmness
on the ball which made him stand out. He just looked old.

At Southampton he gave a very good team a lovely balance
on the left side. He was the last piece of the jigsaw to complete
an outstanding team. We had tried one or two younger lads
down the left but David came along and brought quality to that
position and he fitted in from day one as if he had been with us
all his life. We did not have to teach him a thing because he was
already a great professional and his understanding of the game
and the way we played it was instantaneous.

What a team that Southampton squad of the early 1980s
was. There was already great flair with the likes of Channon
and Ball and one or two others and we beat all the big boys

for fun week after week. No one on the outside expected much of us but the difference was that we, the players, did expect to do well. Players like Dave Watson, Chris Nicholl and the rest of us, getting towards the end of our careers, still wanted to win. There is a subconscious temptation among players of that age and stage to wind down in one last big move but here was a group of players, many of them in their 30s, who were still desperate to succeed. None of us were looking for an easy run and that is why we came so close to winning the First Division.

I have to say we were not quite good enough. One of the reasons, in my view, was that Southampton did not have the volume of support of the bigger clubs. We had tremendous backing home and away, and from the South Coast fans had to travel many costly miles, but the major clubs will always have an advantage in the sheer size of their following and I think that is what counted against us in the final reckoning.

David was a better player than I thought he was going to be, if I am honest. Sometimes when a player joins a club you find out a weakness or two which you had not expected but with David, he did what it said on the tin. Every performance was an eight out of ten, no matter the occasion or location. You always got the same excellence. Above all, in a team of veterans, he worked his socks off, covering huge areas of the pitch to save our older legs. We needed him to do that and he never disappointed.

I am amazed to discover he only got three England caps. I thought he had got a few more than that, as he should have done, and he would have got more today without a doubt. I suppose at the time there were quite a few left-sided players in competition and sometimes it is simply a managerial choice, depending on the way the England team is set up tactically. But I think the most likely cause of his lack of international recognition is that in Middlesbrough and Southampton he played for two unfashionable clubs. It does help to play for the top sides but three caps was poor reward for a player of David's calibre.

David would have been better appreciated now. When he was in his prime the vogue was for bigger players and although he could look after himself he would have got more room, more protection and more freedom. David always had a lovely left foot and although he was not pacy he lacked nothing in courage and being a clever player, he used his guile to drift past opponents and his goalscoring record shows he could finish with the best of them.

I think that if he played now he would have played in a more central midfield role. On the left side he was no winger and no wing-back but centrally the ball would have come to him more often and he knew how to use it. Another of his great attributes was his durability and he seemed to go on for ever. All those many matches in succession for Middlesbrough was ridiculous and I wonder if any other outfielder will again do what he did. Perhaps if he had played more centrally he would have got a few more injuries but to steer clear of anything serious for all those years was an achievement in itself.

Like the way he played, David was always unchanging. He had this great ability to mix with everybody and was an affable and much-liked member of the team, sociable and humorous. I understand he has mentioned further in the book about the ordeal of singing a song for the rest of the squad, a cruel initiation which comes to every new signing at most clubs. He says it was painful but I can assure him it was not nearly as painful as it was for us listening. If David had chosen to make his living as a singer this book would not have been written. Overall he was as reliable off the field as he was on it.

David makes mention of the fearsome five-a-side matches we held at Southampton the day before big games. No other major club in the world would have allowed something as blood-thirsty and as competitive to take place on Fridays when players should have been saving their energy and aggression. When I first joined Southampton I said to Lawrie he should stop these dangerous sessions because I had never seen such ferocity among team-mates, such thunderous tackles and commitment. But after three weeks I was worse than them all. Lawrie said the players wanted it that way. For 25 minutes we all turned into something else. But the amazing thing was no one ever got hurt and injuries were rare. David was always in the thick of it.

I am pleased to be able to write these few words on David's behalf. He was an underestimated, excellent footballer and a good man. He had some bad times after his career finished but he pulled through them and recovered through strength of character and I know his story will be a good one. He deserves the best.

KEVIN KEEGAN
September 2012

Tribute From Jack Charlton

D AVID ARMSTRONG had not played very much for Middlesbrough when I took over as manager but I could see from the first pre-season friendly or two that he was a hell of a good player. David sealed the left side of our midfield from day one and gave the club tremendous service over many years and, like a lot of that team, did not get the individual recognition he deserved.

We had a great team and played to our strengths and the weaknesses of our opponents. We had in Alan Foggon a striker who might have made a living as a sprinter. He was that fast. Teams in those days played offside and our aim was to get David and the great Bobby Murdoch to find the gaps behind defences for Alan to run in to. Alan was not so good with the ball but if we did all the right things he could get on the end of those through balls and put them away.

David was a great passer and a little quicker than people think. He also got more than his fair share of goals from midfield. He was an intelligent player but not a big lad and that might have counted against him in England terms. They always want big lads.

I think back to the lads we had like David Mills, Foggon, John Hickton, Willie Maddren, Stuart Boam and John Craggs and, like David, they either played little for England or not at all. In my view they were all good enough but maybe Middlesbrough didn't capture the imagination of the national media.

David was an important part of an outstanding team and it didn't change much at all from year to year. We should have won a trophy or two. We were certainly good enough.

Looking back, I think I should have stayed as Middlesbrough manager for one more year. It is easy to say that now but when I left we were not far away from winning honours regularly. I left behind a great team and some fine players. David was one of those.

David had a top class domestic career and should have played many more times for England. He was easily good enough.

JACK CHARLTON
October 2012

1

Robson's Dogged Bench-Warmer

FOUR HOURS after playing for England against World Cup finalists West Germany in front of 68,000 at Wembley I was attempting to clean a sheepdog's diarrhoea from a shagpile carpet at my home on the outskirts of Southampton, still clad proudly in my England blazer and tie, the roar of the crowd a distant and dream-like memory. Jevvy, the guilty incontinent dog, appeared unrepentant as I got on my hands and knees, scrubbing furiously while my wife Maureen shouted, 'He's your dog. You clean it up.' The children were upstairs fast asleep, oblivious of the whole horror.

But just as England had been beaten earlier that night, I too was forced to admit defeat. The carpet was never going to be restored by my despairing efforts and a few days later I was forking out £1,500 to replace it. This was October 1982. I was 27, at the peak of my career, an international footballer enjoying the attention and recognition that comes with playing against and with the best players in the world. And yet the shagpile carpet incident was somehow symbolic of my failure to establish myself among the elite. Just when it seemed I had cracked it, something seemed to go wrong and I was always brought tumbling back to earth.

On this occasion, one minute I was playing against Karl-Heinz Rummenigge, Pierre Littbarski and the great Lothar Matthaus at that wonderful sporting arena, the next I was on all fours, covered in dog excrement. I suppose I can say that at least I played for England, albeit a paltry three times. In my, admittedly extremely biased view, it should have been 33 and maybe even more.

Over 16 years, mostly in the top flight, not many players could have matched me for consistency in league terms. I went seven years, all but one in the First Division, at Middlesbrough without missing a game and then spent another six at Southampton where Lawrie McMenemy assembled a side laden with big names that came desperately close to achieving a league and cup double. But a regular England place always eluded me, and to this day it bugs me. From midfield and spread over my time in the game I scored 146 league and cup goals and yet my international appearances at all levels to include a handful of Under-23 and B caps were handed out almost apologetically.

Even the way I gained my first cap was bizarre. It was 1980 and I was flying for Middlesbrough with 14 league and cup goals and getting top-class reviews up and down the country. That year I was named Football Writers' North-East Player of the Year at a ceremony at the Three Tuns in my home city of Durham and it remains one of the proudest nights of my life. To be in the same hall as such North-East football giants of the past like Wilf Mannion, Len Shackleton, George Hardwick and Jackie Milburn was an honour in itself while McMenemy, Southampton's manager but a North-Eastern lad, presented me with my prize.

The flattering clamour for me to be given my England chance grew louder with every performance and the football writers did their part in making sure my name was at the forefront almost on a daily basis. In the end their cry 'Armstrong for England' could not be ignored any longer. There was a B international at Roker Park in March 1980, for which I was chosen, and I would like to think this was on merit, not because it was being staged in the North-East. We won 1-0 and the match itself was uneventful except that I recall the Spaniards made us run around a lot more than I had been used to in the domestic game. There was no doubt that John Neal, the Middlesbrough manager, and before him Jack Charlton would have been pushing my cause but I have a feeling Ron Greenwood, the interim England manager after Don Revie's unseemly departure, didn't rate me in quite the way Revie had done before.

Two months later in May, as England prepared for the European Championships, Greenwood was obliged to select in effect two international teams simultaneously. There was a fixture with Australia to be fulfilled, which became the first full international between the countries after they had asked for it to be upgraded from B status. Middlesbrough were due to fly to Japan to take part in the Kirin Cup and since I was one of the club's major players, Neal asked the England management if I was also likely to be wanted by them in Australia. Much to be my great delight they said I was. The two events clashed but arrangements were made for me to catch up with the rest of the England party in Sydney once my Middlesbrough commitments had been completed.

In fact they weren't completed because we reached the final of the tournament after beating the Chinese national side in the semi and I had to leave almost as soon as the semi-final had been played. I was told instead to get an overnight flight from Tokyo to Sydney where I was to be met and taken to the hotel in Rushcutters Bay. I duly arrived, bleary-eyed early the next morning, a solitary balding Englishman in a plane-load of small Japanese, only to discover there was no one there to greet me. Having waited around long enough to know I had either been missed or forgotten I made my own way to the hotel, arriving there at 8.30am with half the squad nowhere to be seen. At this point a taxi driver, the man deputed to bring me from the airport, showed up to say David Armstrong had not been on the plane. Not exactly a great start, then, and it got worse.

With Greenwood organising the main squad, Bobby Robson was placed in charge for the trip to Australia. Robson was later to become one of the more successful England managers and his achievements at Ipswich, where he had transformed a provincial side into one of the best teams in Europe, were huge. The following year Ipswich won the UEFA Cup and the England hierarchy were obviously testing his credentials in the same way as they were testing mine. Bobby Robson told me I was rooming with his namesake Bryan Robson but not to go to the room yet because he was having a lie-in and was not to be disturbed. So I hung around the foyer until 11am until I was at last able to take up my bags, Bryan having woken and come down for some breakfast. Bryan was a lad from Chester-le-Street, almost my neck of the woods, and with our similar backgrounds we got on well but this was a strange introduction.

Bobby was also from the North-East but that didn't help in any way. I don't think he wanted me there. My selection had been Greenwood's and from that chaotic arrival to the moment I left to go back to Japan, I never felt part of this particular England set-up.

Bobby had this habit of forgetting people's names. To some this would be an endearing trait but to me it was just plain rude. I am told he spent a decade at Ipswich referring to Eric Gates as

Eric Sykes and in our team meeting later that day he welcomed me as 'Chic'. My nickname at Middlesbrough was Spike for reasons I shall explain later and when he said 'Chic has joined us from Japan', I thought he was talking about someone else. But then came the big put-down. 'Chic has come all the way from Japan so I'm going to have to play him,' he said in front of his assembled squad. One minute he tells me I'm in the team, about to make my England debut, surely one of the proudest moments in any player's career, the next he's telling me he is obliged to play me. As the new boy I wanted the security of knowing that I had been picked on merit, because he thought I could do a decent job, not because I had made a big effort to get to Australia. Sympathy was the last thing I needed.

As the meeting broke up Robson beckoned me over, perhaps I thought to give me a few words of much-required assurance as I was about to embark on my inevitably nervous debut. 'By the way Chic,' he confided, 'I have taken your bloody England suit halfway round the world in my suitcase. Come and get it.'

I played on the left of midfield, my club position, and while the Aussies were not as good as they are now they made life difficult enough so that we only won 2-1 with Glenn Hoddle and Paul Mariner getting our goals. We were two goals up in the first 25 minutes with Russell Osman, Terry Butcher and Alan Sunderland also making their debuts and Peter Ward coming on for his first appearance in the 85th minute. I didn't last the whole match, as was the case in my other two internationals, being replaced by West Ham's Alan Devonshire near the end when we were leading 2-0. But at least I could now call myself an international and at 25 I had reason to suppose I could be on the threshold of an exciting future at this level once I had put behind me this awkward start.

Nagging away at the back of my mind though was the feeling that I was not part of all this, that I was not wanted. I kept thinking, 'What am I doing here?' At the end of the game, hands shaken, bath taken, there was no response from Bobby Robson, good or bad, making my sense of being an outsider, my isolation, all the sharper. I don't think they needed me there. My selection, however merited in my own view, was a sop to Middlesbrough and the North-East. Later I thought back to the game and felt I had done an efficient, un-showy job, the sort I did for Middlesbrough every week, but in the absence of any comment I would never know for sure.

The next day was a rest day and the lads did all the tourist bits; trips around beautiful Sydney harbour, buying souvenir toy koalas and kangaroos for kids back home, before the main party departed early the following morning. I was left behind for a flight that evening to Tokyo to resume my club's tournament and was told officials from the Australian FA would see me to my plane. I voiced the concern that my visa may have been used up coming to Australia but the English management were convinced all was in order. They were long gone by the time I sat down to lunch with the Aussies who, when I pressed my point, kindly checked and came back with the news I feared, namely that my visa had indeed expired and with my flight due to depart at 7pm I had about three hours to get another. I had to reach the Japanese embassy by 4pm, which I just managed, so that I could get my passport stamped. I remember running through the streets to the embassy, thinking, 'Is this international football?'

That evening, with my new visa in place, I left Australia believing I had been enduring a nightmare, ending only when I was able to rejoin my Middlesbrough 'family' in time for us to beat Espanyol on penalties in the final, so all was not so bad. There had been no presentation of my first tasselled England cap in Sydney, as I had supposed there might be, no formal recognition of a step up. In fact the cap arrived in the post some time later with a handful of household bills.

To add to the oddness of the whole episode and as a cricket fan, it was curious to be required to play the international on the turf of the famous Sydney Cricket Ground. I looked at the notorious Hill and thought of all the stick England's cricketers had taken over the years from Aussie fans stationed there but in a way it only heightened the surreal aspect to the whole strange adventure.

From then on until the West German match two and a half years later I flirted with the international scene. Flirted is the right word because there was more promise than there was action. I played for England B at Old Trafford in October 1980 against the USA, a match in which Derek Statham got the only goal. It was always a little hard to believe B internationals actually led to anything and have largely now been abandoned. But another major disappointment was still to come.

In 1981 I switched from Middlesbrough to Southampton and began playing in a side which looked as if it might win titles and cups. Alongside Kevin Keegan, Mick Channon, Alan Ball and other big names and internationals, I think it became clear, if it had not been before, I could hold my own with the very best players.

It got to 1982, I was playing as well as at any time in my life in a top class club team and suddenly the World Cup in Spain was upon us. Everyone wants to play in a World Cup and I was certainly no different and I felt my chances of doing so were excellent after my first season at Southampton in which I got 15 league goals and another in the UEFA Cup. I really thought I stood a great chance of going and, as importantly, being able to make a difference. Everything pointed to my inclusion, not least there being a dearth of left-sided midfield players who could score goals. The papers were tipping me for a squad place.

A squad of 40 players was named and two key players, Keegan and the left-sided Trevor Brooking, were struggling to be fit to play in the tournament. There is no doubt Keegan and Brooking were absolutely vital to England's chances of winning, so they were given every chance to get themselves fit. Also in the 40 after much lobbying and touting in the papers was one David Armstrong. And yet when the squad was reduced to 22 I was one of those left out, a terrible blow after my hopes had been raised because I was convinced my time had come.

I had by then served the best part of ten years in the First Division, played in European competition and I like to think I was regarded by team-mates and opponents alike as one of the better left-sided midfield players around. Instead in my position England took Brooking, who was not fit until the last match against Spain, on the basis of his greater experience and I went from elation at my original selection to something approaching disillusion. Graham Rix played on the left and, as we know, England failed to impress, reaching the last 12. I watched every match, genuinely wanting them to win. I am a true patriot and not even my own hurt could change that.

Allowing for the fact that Brooking was a high class player and was deservedly in front of me I still didn't know what I had to do to get into the international squad but I soon discovered I had not been completely forgotten. I have a strong feeling that after the World Cup the influential Lawrie McMenemy had been extolling my capabilities, as Neal and Charlton had done on my behalf before at Middlesbrough. With Bobby Robson now in charge, I was picked in the squad to face Denmark in a European Championship qualifier in Copenhagen. Even then Robson found a way of omitting me when it came to picking the starting 11.

Football is all about opinions of course but I'm bound to say I should have started in Denmark. Danish crowds can be hostile and intimidating to opponents but it would have made no difference to me and I'm afraid it was another opportunity lost. I so nearly got on. Robson at one point told me to get stripped, ready for action but as I hovered around the touchline, indulging in a few warm-up exercises, the moment came and went and I never did get over the white line. Ricky Hill went on instead in the 83rd minute.

There was one major social consolation anyway to having missed out on the 1982 World Cup. The previous year John Oakenfold, a North-East businessman, ran a cricket team in which celebrities such as Allan Wells, Alan Minter and John Conteh took part, each receiving some little recompense for their trouble. We were playing at Corbridge and after I had got 50-odd, John asked me what I wanted and I knew he always had a hospitality box at Royal Ascot. Never having been to a race meeting, I told him a day there would be nice and he agreed.

So in 1982, and me by now being a Southampton player, John was as good as his word and Maureen and I were invited for three days at the famous course to sample one of the grand occasions of the English summer. What was so fortunate was that we met three couples who were to remain our closest friends over some difficult times ahead. There were John and Maureen Wheeler, Harry and Eve Saunders and Roberto and Sheila Mangoni.

Roberto, or 'Bertie' as we came to know him, brought a television to the hospitality box so he could watch Italy in the World Cup and we soon became regular visitors to his restaurant in Camberley, Surrey. When I was a Saints player he used to sponsor me, new shoes after every two goals or maybe a case of top quality Italian wine. He quickly taught me the glory of a good red wine but what I liked about all these people we had met by chance was that they saw through and beyond the fact that I was a prominent First Division footballer and after those days faded forever they stayed loyal. Maureen and I have not forgotten that.

As for the generous Mr Oakenfold, managing director of a company that made false ceilings, the ceilings proved not to be the only thing false about him. So too were his accounts and I went to visit him at Pentonville prison when his embezzling finally caught him up. John 'The Horse' Wheeler stood surety for him but Royal Ascot seemed a long way off.

After the nearly appearance of Copenhagen, I was called up at last for a really big match, that against West Germany a month later. It may have ended a few hours later with me, cloth in hand and a bowl of soapy hot water, but the match itself was an education. A few months earlier the Germans had been playing in a World Cup Final and all their players were high calibre but I have never been worried by big occasions or big players.

For once the management had got it right, I was playing on the left of midfield with Devonshire outside me and Luton's Ricky Hill making his full debut. I was in my best position and involved, I thought, in all our better moves, doing much the same job I had been doing for Southampton, covering our defence when needed, probing for gaps in the German rear-guard and covering plenty of ground. For the only time in my brief international career I felt at home, comfortable in what I was doing and being able to achieve.

I did have one lucky break. In attempting to pass back to Peter Shilton, the ball was intercepted by a German forward only for Shilton to make the save. That sort of fundamental error could have blown the confidence of some players but I soon got over it, refused to hide and got on with my job. I may not have played much at this level but I was not an inexperienced player and it was not as though I had never previously made a mistake in a big match.

As usual, sad to report, I failed to see the match out. We were losing 1-0 when Graham Rix replaced me and we eventually went down 2-1. The incredible Rummenigge, one of the best players in the world at the time, got both German goals and Tony Woodcock scored ours.

Unfortunately the team was not announced until the morning of the match which meant my parents could not get down in time from Durham to see it, which is something I shall always regret because they were as proud as I was and had supported me throughout my life. Maureen and a friend came up from the South Coast so I had some support and at the end of the night we were told by FA officials we could stay overnight at the Hilton Hotel near Wembley. We were already committed to going home to the children and the dog, an action I was of course to regret just as bitterly after we had driven through the night.

At last I felt like an England player and looked forward with optimism to many more opportunities. We may not have won an important friendly but there was no question from any quarter, as I looked at the papers, that I had contributed fully and I went back to Southampton training expecting much more to follow. Instead I had a long, long wait. It was some 19 months in fact before I got my third and last cap.

In the first few months after the West Germany game I was still involved peripherally, enough to keep me encouraged. I was called to the squads to face Russia at Wembley and Scotland at Hampden Park so that I was able still to label myself an England player, rather than a former one.

Maureen and I were married in September 1982 but we had to change the date on one occasion because of my involvement with England, which was slightly ironic, but it was not until May 1984, when I was 29 and beginning to think I had missed my chance, that I got another, final opportunity. Once again, on the basis of the opinions of others, I had been outstanding at club level, scoring 19 goals in the 1983/84 season, making what I regarded as an irrefutable case for inclusion. For once Robson bowed to statistical pressure.

I was convinced I was playing better than ever but convincing others in key England positions was an altogether different task. My template for a good international manager had been Revie, whom I first encountered in my England Under-23 days. At all levels, Revie, now an often derided figure for snatching Arab gold ahead of the England manager's job, had the gift of good man-management, always keeping players involved, always talking to them, inviting them to get-togethers and thanking them for attending. Revie liked me, of that I have no doubt, because he told me he did and even tried to sign me for Leeds when I was a schoolboy. I think I might have been a key player in any club side he managed as an old style inside-left and had he stayed as England's boss I have an inkling that I might have made a much smoother transition from Under-23, to England B and then full international. Mine was instead peppered with setbacks. Jack Charlton, John Neal and McMenemy were always kind enough to say publicly that I was just about the first name on the team sheet and even the reluctant Robson paid a sort of compliment by going on record to say I worked the left side very well.

By the time I was selected to play Wales at Wrexham on 2 May 1984 I was part of a big group of experienced internationals at Southampton, top players like Mick Mills, Mark Wright and Frank Worthington. The big three of Ball, Keegan and Channon had gone but through McMenemy's incredible capacity to attract the best players, Southampton were still thriving and yet, time after time, in those intervening 19 months when England international squads were announced I was being left at home when they all went off to play for their country, like a footballing Cinderella.

The match itself was little short of a disaster, and not just for me. Bobby Robson chose me to play wide on the left, which he should have known was simply not my best position. I am no left-winger and never have been, being short of the pace required for that position, but being a left-winger was pretty much what he asked me to do. Bryan Robson may have been predominantly left-footed but he was a central midfielder and my preferred position was being occupied by John Gregory who I have to say was fortunate to play for England as often as he did. I often wondered why with Bryan Robson's injury record, I was not given the chance to play in his position.

From my point of view this particular match was best forgotten, the debut-making Mark Hughes scoring the only goal, and by the time I came off to be replaced by Luther Blissett we were already losing and I was feeling I could have contributed a lot, lot more. Neither Bobby Robson nor his assistant Don Howe said a word at the end, they did not need to.

Back at Southampton, going about my club business, I thought my international career was over before it had properly started but no, it lingered for another year of hoping and failing, expectations raised and quashed, which leads me to the tour of South America in the summer of 1985.

I still can't think about this particular jaunt without a shake of the head, the sheer disbelief about what happened to me as raw today as it was then. Maybe Bobby Robson wanted to recognise my part in a great season for Southampton, 1984/85, when we had finished fifth. Maybe he was having second or third thoughts about me as a player at the highest level or maybe I was just making up the numbers. I think I was chosen because Bobby was worried about Bryan Robson's perpetual injury problems and he wanted to see if I could handle the tough opposition we were sure to engage in Uruguay, Brazil and Chile.

The prospect of playing those countries on their own pitches in front of their legendarily passionate fans caused me great excitement even after another long hard domestic season at Southampton. To play at Brazil's Maracana Stadium was a schoolboy's dream come true – Pele had been a hero – and after the long flight to Rio de Janeiro I reasoned that I must get another cap somewhere along the line over the three matches.

The sight of the yellow shirts of Brazil will live with me forever but the match will always be remembered as John Barnes's for his fabulous individual goal, weaving past defenders from the halfway line to score. It is shown again and again on television and little wonder. It made the reputation of Barnes and cemented the reputation of Robson in the hearts of the ruling classes at the FA. I often wonder if Robson had wanted me to play like Barnes but he should have known that I was no forward in the accepted sense despite my scoring record. At the end, as an unused substitute, I went on the pitch to swap shirts, coming home with a number 14, although without a name on the back I had no idea to whom it belonged.

And so to Uruguay who were probably the best team in South America at the time and here we lost to much the better outfit. I sat there on the bench wondering if I was going to get a chance, as I had done against Denmark, but Bobby did not so much as look in my direction and another opportunity passed. This led me to believe, not unnaturally, that I was bound to play a not-very-good Chilean side down in Santiago. Robson could surely not omit me for a third time. But he did.

Again I was on the bench, this time itching to get on. Late in the game it was 0-0, a tepid match was going nowhere and time was ticking away. I kept looking at him, thinking that any second he was going to let me have a little run-out if only to justify my air fares. But Robson just sat there on the bench, soaking up the sun and staring ahead. The final whistle blew and I realised I had travelled thousands of miles for nothing. Barnes, on the back of his wonder goal, played every minute of the tour. Baffled and perplexed I headed home to England, my international career over at 30.

A few years later and by now on Bournemouth's books I was at Lilleshall attempting to overcome a serious ankle injury which was to end my playing days. I noticed Bobby Robson was in residence and decided to confront him, something I might have done earlier I suppose, to find out just why he never picked me in my best position or so infrequently. England never saw the best of me and I wanted to know what it was he had against me or what sort of player he thought I was. Did he see me as a lesser Bryan Robson? Or as a flying winger? He must have known I was none of those and yet my domestic record stood comparison with any.

In my view, and I know it was shared by knowledgeable people within the game, a meagre haul of uncompleted international appearances, a few squad selections and that ludicrous tour of South America was poor reward for what I had to offer. I wanted an answer. When I caught up with him I just hoped he wouldn't preface his response by calling me Chic. Admittedly he didn't do that but he quickly dismissed my argument without providing any real clue as to his thinking. 'I gave you your chance and you did not take it,' he said. I beg to differ. I don't think he ever did. So there it was; three caps and a shagpile carpet later, England was unfulfilled history for me.

2
From England To The Dole

FOUR YEARS after playing for England I was on the dole. I hated the process of signing on. The embarrassment and the humiliation of being unemployed was always hard to take but I never had an alternative. Since my football career was ended by injury after a handful of games at Bournemouth in 1988 I have been forced to sign on three or four times, the players' union, the PFA has helped pay my mortgage and the ex-players' association at Middlesbrough has contributed to one of the many operations I have been obliged to undergo to cure a crippling ankle problem which has left me partially disabled.

After I had last gone on to the dole in August 2011 I was so miserable I wrote down in large black capital letters just how I felt. These were the words: HELPLESS, HOPELESS, WORTHLESS, USELESS, DISAPPOINTED, EMBARRASSED, LET YOURSELF DOWN PERSON-ALLY, LET OTHER PEOPLE DOWN, HURT, SAD, WORRIED.

I have kept that bit of paper as a reminder of just how desperate life could become, how desperate it became once the glamour of my life as a footballer was brought to an abrupt halt. One minute I was a celebrity, the next just another ex-player fallen on hard times, not the first to do so and not the last. A lot of people are on the dole in these days of austerity and I can relate to them.

I can't pretend things have been easy since I was forced into premature retirement, my capacity forever limited by a severely damaged left ankle, the residue of which means I need the helping hand of a £31.62 weekly industrial accident payment and the knowledge that I can never be involved again in football, the only way of life I know anything about. The worst part is that dole queue. I am not exactly unrecognisable with my bald pate and having played for Southampton and England and living in the area for the best part of 30 years, going down to Eastleigh, my nearest signing-on point, has been a deeply hurtful experience. The man behind the desk asks for your name and you wait for a flicker of recognition and even if it doesn't come, you still think they know who you are.

You also have that unnerving feeling that everyone else is looking at you, whispering, sniggering, 'What's he doing here?' I may of course be long forgotten by those who once cheered me from The Dell terraces but the suspicion was always when I went to sign on that they knew who I was.

There was one awful occasion, and I shudder even now to recall it, when I didn't even have enough cash to get to the dole to get my weekly payment. At such moments I wondered what my life had come to. Having to join a dole queue was bad enough, having to ask the PFA and friends at Middlesbrough for money was beyond degrading but, my options were strictly limited. In reality there were no options. I had to ask for money and it's a regret I shall take with me to my old age.

The fact that I'm classed as partly invalid is all the more ironic because I went through my career without injury blemish year after year. Maybe I played too much, preferring to carry injuries from match-to-match hoping they would go away. They often did. Most players of my era did the same, buttressed by the omnipresent painkilling cortisone, and paying for it in later life when, like me, they were forced to hobble painfully.

Racking up more than 700 matches I only ever had one serious injury for the majority of it, needing 17 stitches in my left ankle when playing for Middlesbrough after it had been opened up in a clash with Geoff Palmer of Wolves in an FA Cup quarter-final in March 1981. Nowadays I would have been substituted immediately by anxious coaching staff. But three decades ago they simply strapped it up and sent me back out again. I even created the equaliser for Terry Cochrane and then played in the replay a few days later with it heavily bandaged and in front of 41,000 people. It never occurred to me or to the staff that I might be rested to allow it to heal. I do remember Lawrence Dunne, the club doctor, saying he needed a brandy when he first saw the extent of the injury, sliced as it was to the bone.

Later at Middlesbrough during that long run of consecutive appearances I had some routine x-rays one pre-season where it was revealed I had been playing for years on a fractured left ankle. To this day I have no idea how I got it, not the Palmer tackle for sure, but I just played on, through the so-called pain threshold, so that it mended itself. Was this, though, the precursor for the problems later?

Some six or seven years later, playing for Southampton against Arsenal, I was hurt in a collision with David Rocastle in November 1986. Rocastle went off but I carried on as usual although the more the game progressed I realised I had again damaged the left ankle. I was sent for an x-ray and the verdict was a flaked bone and slight ligament damage. There was nothing to worry about, or so I thought, even if it meant – for me – an unprecedented long absence. When I began playing again six weeks later I told our physio, Don Taylor, I was still in pain but the club's medics said it was merely the bone healing. I even went on tour after the season ended to Singapore and played in every game but at that time, as I shall explain later, I was in dispute with Southampton over a new contract and left in the summer of 1987 without the injury clearing up or being properly diagnosed. I signed instead for Southampton's near neighbours, Bournemouth, then managed by Harry Redknapp.

When I made that list of how I felt at going on the dole, when it came to letting other people down, Harry was one of those I felt I had let down. I very much wanted to play for him. He was building a good Second Division side and there was an optimism about him and around Dean Court which suggested he could, as he suggested to me, get the club into the First Division. I was flattered by him and by the way he came to my house, walked with me around the fields at the back of my garden and told me what he planned to achieve and how he was going to do it. I duly signed a two-year contract and although the ankle was hurting when I walked, I believed I was young enough and fit enough to become the first outfield player to reach 1,000 first class appearances. I was about 200–300 short and at 32 I felt I had plenty of time to reach my target.

In joining Bournemouth I did not have a medical as such. I think they merely looked at my record of appearances over 15 or 16 years and figured there was no need. Medicals were in any case not as stringent or as detailed as they are now and I'm not sure the problem would have been picked up even if they had insisted I had one. The shame is that I enjoyed my short career at Bournemouth and we were briefly, right at the start of the season, second in the table, about as good as it ever got for them. I even scored three goals, one of them against Birmingham, but after half a dozen appearances to include friendlies and with the season still young, we went down to Exeter for a Littlewoods Cup match and it was there that my career effectively came to an end.

There was a moment, a tackle, by no means malicious or ill-intended, which I came out of realising that I had sustained something out of the ordinary. My great friend Bobby Kerr, the man who lifted the FA Cup aloft for Sunderland in 1973 after they had so famously beaten Leeds, had been staying with me and had travelled to Exeter to watch the game. When we got back to Bournemouth on the team coach Bobby had to drive my car home through the New Forest because I could not put my foot down on the clutch. I sat in the passenger seat coming to terms with the grim realisation that my ankle had had enough and that my career might well be over.

I soldiered on briefly, making my final appearance before surgery on 5 September 1987 at Hull where we lost 2-1. For all my difficulties, even in walking, I played in every minute of seven matches in 21 days, but the ankle just would not keep me going any longer. More's the pity because at that time in beating Exeter over two legs we had won through the Littlewoods Cup to play against my old club Southampton in the next round. How I would have loved to have played at The Dell again, if only to prove a point or two to some key people there, in particular the manager, Chris Nicholl. Bournemouth went on to create something of an upset by beating the First Division side 3-2 on aggregate and I only wish I hade been able to play some part in the triumph. Instead I had already been in for my first operation and listened to both matches on the radio while contemplating my future.

While my Bournemouth team-mates were deservedly enjoying the victory, one of the best in their recent history and all the sweeter for it coming against local rivals, I was visiting a consultant – and not before time. When I did, I got a shock. The consultant went through my medical history and wanted to give me an x-ray under induced stress but there was no need for stress-induction because I was already in severe discomfort. He said there were problems dating from the Rocastle incident but the Exeter tackle had finally finished me off. Had Southampton sent me for a scan, as they should have done, the previous November after that Arsenal match, it would have shown, as I was now to discover, that I had been attempting to play on with a completely severed ligament. No wonder I had been in pain.

There was nothing else that could be done without surgery so I went under the knife for the first of five or six operations spread over many years during which I often considered at low moments if I should need a stick or some kind of assistance just to go about my daily business. With Redknapp having to get by without his star summer signing, I was having a new ligament inserted with tissue hacked from another part of my leg. There was not ever much chance of coming back from major surgery like that, but even now there is no what they call articular lining and the red scars, criss-crossing the ankle, some as livid as the day they cut me open, look not unlike a badly-drawn road map.

I deeply regret not being able to help Redknapp and fulfil his vision for myself and the team. Redknapp has of course gone on to manage at the highest domestic level and came so close to leading the national team and I can see why. He had this ability to speak in layman's terms, no tactical overload, to everybody – players, fans, press, directors – in the same easy-going, unassuming manner. There were many of the man-management qualities in him which I also found in McMenemy. As long as you gave them 100 per cent on the pitch, they would look after you and treat you properly.

In both cases, McMenemy and Redknapp, they knew how to get the best out of disparate talents and backgrounds and weld them into a coherent team and unit. Redknapp liked footballers, which may sound a little odd, and wanted them to get the best out of themselves and in return he got the respect of the players who were keen to perform for him. Believe me, not all dressing rooms are behind the manager and not all managers are respected by their players. Redknapp wanted you to enjoy your football and that included in training from Monday to Saturday.

We went home with a smile on our faces but, make no mistake, Harry was ambitious and you knew that he would eventually move on from Dean Court when the opportunity arose even though he never appeared in any hurry to leave what I suspect we both considered to be a nice, happy, family club.

At the time of my injury, I was settled on the left side of midfield, proving to myself and others that I could still make some useful contributions in that position. To my great annoyance I had previously been playing at left-back, against my will, at Nicholl's Southampton and the change when I went to Bournemouth was starting to breathe new life into my career, as I hoped it would.

The same consultant told me my career was over. The ankle, even after the initial operation, was still not functioning without it hurting and when I went to see him I knew what was coming. To save myself from further unnecessary punishment he told me it would be best I retired. I didn't put up a fight. There was no point even if I thought I knew what I was about to lose. This was 1988 and it was all over at the age of 33. I had made a brief, desultory attempt at a comeback but my final game was at home to Barnsley in March 1988 and even then I had to be substituted. It could have been worse, I suppose, I might have had the same conversation with the consultant at 24 or even 17 and at least I had a career to look back on.

The problem was that I was convinced I had more to give and that I was still some distance away from a natural conclusion. But that was it. I hobbled out of his consulting rooms not knowing what lay ahead and, with a young family to feed, more than a little fearful of the future. The feeling I most remember of that time, strangely, was of letting people down. I had signed for two years and all Bournemouth could do was pay me up after a year in which I hadn't played much and wish me well. It was then that I first went on the dole, struggling to get through the job centre door so excruciating was the pain, to the extent that I could not even stand up for more than a minute or two at a time.

I had no idea what to do. My ambition was to be a player-coach somewhere, maybe a player-manager to learn my trade so that one day I could become a full-blown manager, but it didn't take a genius to work out that no one was going to give a job to a guy so crippled he couldn't put any weight on his damaged ankle. To get anywhere in football I was going to need a coaching certificate so I did at least get that started, studying for my FA full badge at Aberystwyth under Jimmy Shoulder, who had brought Ryan Giggs through, and only myself, David Giles and Osher Williams came away from the course qualified.

I had always been interested in coaching, attending one in Durham City in 1979 organised by George Wardle. But, truth to tell, I was running out of money from my pay-off by the time Bournemouth threw me a lifeline, making me their football in the community development officer, a post created jointly by the PFA, the FA and the Football League, which at least kept me involved in football without paying nearly as well as when I was a player. There was no doubt I was going to have to get used to a much-diminished lifestyle.

Working with the Dorset FA, going down to Weymouth and Dorchester and such places, I learned quickly about other aspects of football, the importance of projecting a public profile, of meeting people and raising money.

All was going well until Redknapp left for West Ham in 1992. I applied for his job in the belief that as an ex-player to a high level and after learning more about another side to the game in my present position I was perfectly qualified. The manager's position went instead to his coach, Tony Pulis, on Redknapp's recommendation, which left me distinctly vulnerable. Pulis, who of course eventually followed Redknapp into the Premier League, was not going to be happy to think that within Dean Court was a man who also thought he could do his job. So within days of his appointment I went to see him to reassure him of my support and to point out I had no desire to be his rival in any way. I told him I didn't want him to see me as a threat because I was happy minding my own business in my job in the community office.

Pulis was in his first managerial role and had been given the task of reducing a massive wage bill left behind by Redknapp. It was not going to be an easy task and by 1997 the debts were so big the club was famously within 15 minutes of folding. By then I was long gone. In fact I was gone within three weeks of my meeting with Pulis.

Luckily, and I needed some luck, a job similar to that I had been doing at Bournemouth came up at Reading and I snapped it up gratefully. Reading were not then Premier League material, as they are now, and were playing at homely Elm Park in the centre of town, a club in size not unlike Bournemouth with much the same level of ambition until wealthy businessman Sir John Madejski and his money came along. I fancied the challenge, knew what the job entailed and worked contentedly alongside managing director Mike Lewis.

Mark McGhee was the Reading manager at the time and through Reading and the PFA I gained a further qualification, an NVQ assessor's badge and the urge to get involved on the playing side remained as strong as ever.

It was always hard, as an ex-player, to spend the week working at a stadium for a club and then not to be part of what happened on the Saturday when the place was alive and the adrenaline was flowing. Not long into my time at Elm Park McGhee left and was replaced by the joint managership of Jimmy Quinn and Mick Gooding. It was a brave move by the chairman, putting two senior professionals in charge of players who had been their pals and contemporaries but it worked for a time.

Quinn, a former Northern Ireland international striker, and the experienced Gooding knew I was in the building and they knew of my background. One day they asked me if I would like to get involved on the playing side again, do some coaching, work with individual players, that sort of thing. In many respects this was just what I had been looking for and working towards with my badges but deep down I knew it couldn't possibly work. The reason was my sore, swollen and carved-up ankle, gnawing away at me, dogging my every step. There were times when it was so painful even a bed sheet placed upon it hurt as much as if someone had taken a hammer to it.

Quinn and Gooding were insistent I tried and try I did. In one match against Wolves I was invited into the dressing room before the start to give a little talk and help prepare the team for the battle ahead. For a wonderful few hours I was back in the environment I understood, loved and craved, back among footballers on a match day, carried along by the smell of liniment in the nostrils and the excited banter of the players. How I wished at that moment I was still playing. But then reality kicked in, the realisation that there was no way I could sustain a coaching role in my state of disability. How could I have worked with players on the training ground every day of the week when I was barely able to walk? So I had to be honest with the managers. There was a job offer on the table and all I had to do was say I wanted it and it was mine. But I went to Quinn and Gooding and told them that, much as I would have relished such an opportunity, I was going to have to turn it down.

It was a heartbreaking decision to have to make, but it was best to be honest because I knew I could not have partaken in any kind of physical activity on the training pitch, however peripheral, and in the long term I would have been letting people down if I had accepted. At the back of my mind, though, was always the belief that I would one day be fit enough for such a role. Indeed I still reckoned I could do some kind of job on the playing side, somewhere, as long as it didn't involve any running around.

For that reason I must have applied for around 50 jobs as manager, as a scout and in commercial departments. The nearest I got to a manager's job at that time was at Scarborough when they were still in the league. I was called for a 5pm interview and as I pulled into the car park after a long drive I saw Andy King, the former Everton player and Swindon manager, coming out. He stopped long enough to tell me that according to the local paper the next manager was going to be Steve Wicks who had already been appointed. I duly went into the interview expecting to be told to turn round and go home but the courteous board of directors never mentioned Wicks and I had a good interview, leaving with hope renewed. But, sure enough, Wicks did get the job, lasting ten matches before quitting. I like to think I could have brought much more to the table, so to speak, had I been made manager. My background was North-Eastern, I had lots of contacts in the game who might have come to us for money-earning friendlies and I knew how to raise money from my time in commercial departments, especially in finding top class speakers for dinners.

Mike Lewis, who had been acting as a consultant to the Southern League club Waterlooville, got me a job there as general manager, which I considered to be a step up because I was in effect running the club, and despite it being in the Portsmouth area, my Southampton links were never a hindrance. It was closer to home for a start and I was responsible for the whole of the funding in all the usual ways plus putting on sportsman's dinners at which Jack Charlton and Duncan McKenzie were among the guest speakers.

Billy Gilbert, the former Crystal Palace and Portsmouth defender, was manager and it was soon clear that no matter how much money I raised it was never going to be enough to cover costs, not least the huge wages paid to part-time professional players. The more I shovelled in through sponsorship, advertising boards, holiday coaching courses and after-school clubs, the more it disappeared the other end into Billy's playing budget. It was not Billy's fault because he had to pay the going rate, often for players who had never been near a Football League club and never would. It was inevitable it couldn't continue and eventually Waterlooville merged with nearby Havant to become Havant and Water- looville but by then I had left without ever being able to fill the financial gap.

From there I dropped to the Wessex League in a full-time post of commercial manager of Lymington and New Milton. It was not ever going to be ideal but I had a mortgage to pay and mouths to feed and the most I could do was to make sure our house, the one remnant of my more prosperous playing days, was not repossessed, as it so nearly was on one occasion.

I was surprised to learn that even at this much-reduced level players were being paid and again with more money than I could ever expect to bring in for them. To be honest the players were not a great deal better than fit parks-pitch players and New Milton had been obliged to merge with neighbouring

Lymington for financial and facility reasons. This is of course the big problem in football at all levels, the money generated off the pitch never adequately covers wages. I don't blame players for getting as much out of the game in terms of wages as they can because as I knew to my cost, it's a short life. But you shouldn't expect to pay wages at places like New Milton.

Around that time I was doing a little coaching in the evenings with local league clubs in the Southampton area like Colden Common and Netley, and Trevor Parker, in charge at Bashley of the Southern League, asked me to help him. I agreed on one condition, that he paid my expenses because I couldn't afford the petrol from my home at Fair Oak to Bashley in the New Forest, all of 25 miles away. Things were that bad. Parker talked about a full-time job if we got promotion and when we were promoted I waited for him to carry out his promise. I am still waiting.

All the while my ankle was causing me agony. From that first operation in 1987 to the sixth and hopefully last in June 2011 I endured continual misery. It blighted my life and prevented me from fulfilling what I believe was my destiny within the game but the old 'war wound' wouldn't let me. Only now can I walk properly thanks to the skills of surgeons but even then only cautiously. I have to watch every step because I have re-adapted the way I get about and it's not easy or natural. I have to check the surface I walk on in case there are dips and bumps, I need to turn with care and I will never, ever be able to run again.

Even allowing for a healthy appetite, the result of my lack of movement is that I now weigh something in the region of 16 and a half stone, which for a man of 5ft 7ins is, I admit, far too much. I had an endoscopy, arthroscopy and operations to clean out the crystallised, flaked bone within. Eventually I was told the ankle required fusing and I shall be forever thankful to the PFA and the Middlesbrough Ex-Players' Association for helping with the funding. Pitifully, there was no way I could have afforded it on my own.

Sadly, after going to both organisations and begging for their help, I knew straight away the surgery hadn't worked. For three months I was obliged to keep my plastered foot off the ground, knowing deep down that the operation had been a failure. I lay on my sofa every day for three months in a state of despair and only the support of my family and friends I had mentioned earlier got me through this daily crisis. The highlight of those endless days was watching a woodpecker coming to my garden to feed off the lawn and the bag of nuts put out each day by Maureen. I envied the bird's mobility.

The reason the operation was a failure was because I had been prescribed, as it transpired, the wrong sort of anti-inflammatory drugs. Luckily, it being a medical mistake there was a duty of care which meant the same surgeon, Dr Uglow, an acknowledged expert in ankle problems, carried out a further operation at the Spire Hospital in Southampton on the NHS. This one, I am massively relieved to report, worked and now I can actually walk pain-free for the first time since I did the damage at Exeter all those years ago. To put it in perspective, the victory is a small one. The ankle may not hurt any more but there is no joint in it and I have no flexibility, although I consider this a small price I have happily paid for the simple pleasure of getting about.

What I did lose was the years when I might have been playing with the children, the middle years of my life when I could have been far more vigorous than I was. The industrial accident award, however meagre it might seem, has been a help over the years and came after an appeal not long after I had finished playing but there was a stage when we were living hand-to-mouth and every little bit has been appreciated. Had that last operation failed again the next option was to drill two holes in the sole and insert yet more pins. Thankfully it never came to that. As it is, I have enough metal in the foot to set off airport alarms every time I go through them. There's no need to take off my belt.

The outcome is that my whole life was ruined by a football injury. It messed up what I thought would be a natural progression through the world I knew best. Had I not been such an invalid I would have concluded my playing career two or three years later than I did and then moved upwards since my background should have opened doors. But I adapted and so too did my family.

My lowest point was lying on that sofa in my sitting room, bored, fearful, out of work and in silent pain. There was a dark moment when I seriously considered cutting off the bottom part of my leg, but it soon passed. At my wit's end I said to Maureen, 'I don't need it.'

There was many a night when I cried myself to sleep. I guess I was feeling sorry for myself but it was all a million miles from Wembley and the recognition of fans across the country. I am glad they never saw me in such an agonised state. Fame of any kind is wonderful while it lasts in a seductive sort of way but we all know of sportsmen who like me fell on hard times. I am so pleased mine are over but it was a wretched journey.

3

Following George To Middlesbrough

O
NE OF my England shirts I gave to George Wardle, an imposing former military physical training instructor to whom I owed so much. George was my mentor, inspiration and guide through the formative early years of my career and by giving him the shirt it was a gesture of the esteem which I held him and to thank him for all he had done for me. George is long dead and the shirt now resides with his son, Colin, and I would like to think it means something to him and his family. I know George was quietly delighted when I gave it to him but he was not the sort to show great emotion.

George was the principal reason I joined Middlesbrough as a nine-year-old and the man who instilled in me personal discipline, fairness, professionalism and respect for authority, all qualities which seem vaguely old-fashioned now but which were the cornerstone of my 20 years in the game. When I knew him, he was an FA staff coach in the North-East and was teaching in my home city at Durham Technical College. George played a single game in 1937/38 for Middlesbrough before the Second World War and then afterwards appeared for Exeter, Cardiff, QPR and Darlington as an outside-right but, like so many, the conflict cut through what would have been the best years of his own playing days and when those ended he concentrated on developing the careers of others as an exemplary teacher.

Through his courses at Houghall he brought through the system people like Howard Wilkinson and built a reputation as an exceptional coach with firm ideas about the way the game should always be played. One of his great achievements was to lead Crook Town to an FA Amateur Cup triumph over Enfield at Wembley in 1964, although the team was actually picked by a committee of 12, and I count myself fortunate to have come under his influence.

As a child growing up in Durham you supported Sunderland or Newcastle, both of which were within striking distance, and yet the fact that I ended up 35 miles away at Middlesbrough had a lot to do with George and his persistence. If I'd had a choice as a child I would have signed for my beloved Sunderland but their interest in me was never obvious, if indeed it existed. Leeds and Burnley also wanted me when it became clear I had some talent, but not Sunderland it appeared even though I was right on their doorstep. In fairness to all of those clubs I was committed to Middlesbrough thanks in the main to Wardle from an early age and I never really wanted to play for any other club once I had made my choice.

I guess George must have read the local paper, the *Durham Advertiser*, a little more thoroughly than most because through schools matches my name was appearing on a regular basis and from there I must have been attracting attention. Every Tuesday and Thursday, George used to drive myself and another player of promise, Malcolm Smith, to Middlesbrough for evening training and coaching. I would get the bus home from grammar school, do some homework, have some tea and then go with George and Malcolm, who was from Ferryhill, to Ayresome Park for our sessions. Then he would drive us home and at 9pm, drop me off outside Bell's fish and chip shop on Sunderland Road. I would treat the family to fish and chips before sitting down to finish my homework. That routine went on until I was 15 and ready to join the club's academy.

Through it all George was unwavering in his support and his belief in me, teaching me to play football in what he knew – and I came to know – to be the correct manner. From the start he would not tolerate any kind of cheating; no feigned injuries, no disputing refereeing decisions, no malicious tackles, no off-the-ball retribution. It was a man's game and he wanted us to act like men. When I was playing for Middlesbrough's youth team it was not uncommon when he was in charge for us to finish the match with ten or even nine players. If he thought any of his team was in any way not playing the game properly he would take them off the pitch, no matter the score, no matter how important the occasion. He hated any kind of answering back, any disrespect and I think all of us benefited from George's iron rule because we learned the hard way what we needed to do to become professional footballers.

I had in any case also learned many of those disciplines from my parents. My dad, Jack, was a painter and decorator and my mam, Nora, was a dinner lady, working for a time at Durham's ice rink. They had a large family, six of us in total, and both worked in a nightclub to add to the family income. My eldest brother Billy was the musical one of four boys and two girls, with an ability to play the guitar. John, who is now dead, and Joseph were good amateur players in the Northern League, which was a high standard. John rejected the chance of a trial with Darlington, probably because a footballer's pay in those days, particularly in the lower divisions, was not very high and it was an insecure way of making a living. I was the youngest of the four boys and we were followed by our two sisters, Jeanette and Susan, who loyally watched me play up and down the country later, travelling at great personal cost to all kinds of obscure places as well as the big stadia over many years.

I was small for my age, which meant I had to look after myself quickly on the football pitch, so that when I eventually headed for Middlesbrough they could see I could cope with any physical challenge posed by larger lads. I loved my childhood even though it was spent in rough, tough areas, such as the notorious Sherburn Road estate in Durham – a bit of a no-go area for the police – and later the Sunderland Road estate in Gilesgate.

As children, we were always playing football, morning and night, on a strip of land called Duff Heap or the Duffy as we kids knew it. It really was jumpers-for-goalposts, the phrase used by Ron Manager in *The Fast Show*, with up to 20 of us kicking the ball backwards and forwards until we were called in by our parents for tea. Then we were back out in alleys or playing under lampposts. Two of my pals at the time were Stephen Forster and George Maddox who lived opposite me in Bradford Crescent and I keep in touch with George even now, as I did with him all through my playing career. There was a big community feel about the area, everyone knew each other and no one felt the need to lock their back door.

I suppose it was typical of industrial, northern England of that era, the early 60s, with parents doing their best in difficult circumstances to raise a family, working what seemed to me to be all hours while we children were oblivious of their struggles, if not playing football then down in the woods getting up to all kinds of mischief. Looking back, I owe them a great debt of gratitude because I sailed through my childhood with nothing but happy memories. My dad even bought me my first football boots; high-sided, brown and round-toed, they look more like rugby boots but they retain pride of place in my trophy cabinet, a reminder of the sacrifices they made to ensure all of us children got the best of what they could afford.

The great motivating force throughout my playing career was those people I had left behind in the North-East. In effect I played for them as much as I played for myself. I was an outstanding player from a very early age and I say that without bragging because that was the truth. Later, as I progressed into the professional ranks and beyond, I was mindful every time I played of my contemporaries, those lads who had not been blessed, as I had, with a natural talent and who would have loved to be in my position, playing in parts of the world they could only have dreamed about and with and against household names. I was privileged.

There is of course an arbitrary aspect as to why one person is brilliant at something and others not and so it was with me at football. George Maddox was one of those from my home territory who followed my career, not with envy, but pride. They wanted me to do well for them and it was always very humbling to think of that, of how fortunate I had been to be singled out. There was never an occasion on a professional pitch when I didn't feel a sense of responsibility to everyone back at home. I wanted them to feel proud of me, to see that I was carrying their banner, so to speak, into battle. That is one of the reasons why I was only ever booked twice and why I largely stayed out of trouble.

I used to go back to Durham to visit family and would be stopped in the streets by people I didn't know to say how pleased they were for me and how they were rooting for me to succeed. There was never any resentment or jealousy but what helped drive me on to play for England was the knowledge that I was representing the community where I had grown up, the lads on the Duffy and their families. I vividly recall lining up before the start of the West German game, as I say, probably the pinnacle of my career, and thinking of those knockabout games with the other lads. I lived my career for them.

I first became aware that I was different, exceptional even, at a very early age when teams were being drawn up on the Duffy. I was always one of the first chosen even though I was small and younger than most of the participants but my extra ability put me in demand. In many ways the experience of carrying lesser players toughened me physically, because opponents tried every way to stop me, and mentally I often thought how much those battles on the Duffy shaped my attitude in later life, making me far more responsible and team-orientated than perhaps I might have been in what can be a selfish sport. On the rough-hewn scrapping field of the Duffy it was impossible to get above yourself.

The North-East has always been a traditional breeding ground for top footballers with an endless list of top class talent always emerging from some part of it. In recent years there have been Alan Shearer and Paul Gascoigne and now Andy Carroll seems to be following a long and impressive list of outstanding footballers. Not many, if any, other areas of England can claim so many great players per head of population. Football scouts are a hardy breed, hugging touchlines of obscure schools matches in all weathers to look for the great players of tomorrow, like digging for gold and so it was in my day with the likes of Jack Hixon and George Wardle, competing talent-spotters, trawling the North-East for future stars.

Hixon had a spell at Southampton later, sending down Shearer among many, but he worked for Burnley when I was growing up and had sent them prospective England players like Ralph Coates and Dave Thomas. When I was nine, the scouts started to knock at our door, asking my dad to let me go and train. Burnley, Don Revie's Leeds and Newcastle were the most active but there was nothing from Sunderland to whom, as I say, I was devoted. I watched their every home game at

Roker Park and a few away, travelling with my cousin William on a bus from West Auckland.

Health and Safety would have apoplexy now but there was an occasion when Manchester United visited a packed Roker that I was passed down over the heads of the crowd on to the track so that I could see the game. It was not uncommon. I think that day I lost William but gained a love of the wonderful game, resolving that soon I should play it and preferably for Sunderland. My heroes were the indomitable Irish defender Charlie Hurley, the cultured Scottish midfield player Jim Baxter and that great goalkeeper Jim Montgomery whose save in the 1973 FA Cup Final against Leeds is replayed almost as often as Gordon Banks's against Brazil. But I can reel off the names of the rest of the team with just as much ease; George Mulhall, George Herd, Len Ashurst, Cec Irwin and Joe Baker, all admired from my place on the terraces of the Roker End.

As I became better at playing the game my viewing of it became less frequent. I was soon playing for school, district and county, encountering the likes of Brian Little, Alan Kennedy and his brother Keith and a big striker called Chris Guthrie, all of whom played league football. It truly was a hot-bed of talent. I like to think Sunderland knew about me but it was not to be because George Wardle had done enough to persuade me that I should join Middlesbrough and I never regretted it. Later I got to play at Roker Park, which was an ambition fulfilled, but I always wanted to excel against Sunderland, which generally I did, as if I was settling a grudge. As for the dreaded Newcastle, whom I loved to hate, my only two bookings (both for fouls) came playing against them which must say something about my deep-seated desire to get the better of the Magpies.

The fact that I had pledged myself to Middlesbrough did not seem to placate other clubs or dampen their desire to lure me from Ayresome Park. Hixon was particularly persevering and Leeds were competitive to the last. In the end I gave way and went to both clubs on trial, just to look them over. Revie wanted me to join them and of course it was tempting and flattering but I was a bit of a home bird and I asked myself if I wanted to move and twice I said no. I am sure I made the right choice but the presence of George Wardle at Middlesbrough was an important factor in that decision.

Had I not been a footballer, might I have been a chorister? I doubt it, but certainly the choir at St Nicholas' Church in the market place in Durham played a significant role in my childhood. As a boy soprano I was obliged to attend practice every Tuesday and Thursday at one stage, before football took over, earning the princely sum of one old pre-decimal penny for each session and tuppence for a Sunday service. My father was a churchman and I think he was just pleased that one of us boys had joined a choir but my attendance might now be seen as purely professional, earning just about enough extra pocket money to buy something relating to football.

Bobby Charlton and Pele were my great heroes. I loved Bobby's style and it helped that he was a North-Eastern boy but above all, as Wardle was keen to point out, he conducted himself so impeccably on the pitch. We all wanted to be Bobby Charlton.

I loved cricket too. In those days we kids played cricket on the Duffy in the summer months and I went on to play a decent standard for Durham as an all-rounder. In those days Durham were not members of the County Championship so there was no route there but another PE teacher, Mr Brown, always told me that I could have been at least as good a cricketer if I had chosen that sport in preference, but by then I knew what I intended to do with my life.

Academically I had to work hard to achieve what little I did, showing some aptitude for maths, geography and physical education but football always dominated my school years. In fairness there were teachers right from the age of five who encouraged me to develop my skills in the game, not least Mr Chadwick at my first school, Blue Coat School in Durham, before I moved on to Gilesgate New Junior School which was 100 yards from where I lived.

The problem there was that we did not at the start have a football team at Gilesgate; of the six or seven lads there I was the only one who could kick a ball in a straight line. Eventually we got a team up and lost in a cup final to the Blue Coat School. Alan Suddick, the Newcastle footballer, presented the trophy and I cried all the way through the ceremony, bitterly disappointed at our failure. By a strange irony, Suddick later joined Blackpool and I made my debut against him for Middlesbrough. At the age of 11, and by now very much attached to Middlesbrough, I played in another final, the Minto Cup when we beat the Tin School, as it was known. It was at that age also that there was a twist in my education which might have led me on a different path.

Sapere Aude, dare to be wise, was the Latin motto of Durham Johnston Grammar School whose list of prominent old boys is made up of worthy lawyers, medical men and high-powered businessmen. But not footballers. My elder brother Billy passed the 11+ but decided not to go there, preferring nearby Whinney Hill School. I passed the entrance exam and the headmaster at Gilesgate, Mr Thomson, and the sports masters, Michael Henderson, a well known local referee, and Mr Wyatt decided the school would benefit me and in so many ways they were right. The grammar school also emphasised the qualities of decency, fairness, hard work and determination. I loved it but never took to rugby, much as I now enjoy the game, preferring it in so many ways to football as a game to watch, although I can't pretend to understand the finer points. I was a poor tackler as a footballer but even worse when playing rugby, once being sent off in a PE game for attempting to bring down an opponent with my feet.

Rugby teaches you a lot including not to show the world if you are hurt and to accept physical punishment without complaining. Those are some of the aspects I admire about rugby now and would like to see in football but, if anything, the Premier League has gone the other way with its divers and moaners. But we did have an exceptional football team, considering it was essentially a rugby school, and we hammered all our opponents mercilessly. We likened ourselves to the great Real Madrid side of the time with Di Stefano, Puskas and Gento, in our minds at least.

While I was no scholar, I loved the grammar school and the teaching of John Doyle and Joe Robson, a polio victim. When I was selected for England Under-23s at the age of 20, definitely a first for the school, Robson was kind enough to write a letter, which I have treasured along with another from Bill Bagley, the grammar school headmaster and a committed rugby man, expressing their delight at my achievement. Mr Robson wrote, 'You have absolutely no idea how proud I am to have had you in my team and it really is a great thrill for me every time I read about you or see something on TV about you.'

What embarrasses me slightly is the knowledge that they never knew I was training with Middlesbrough at the time and that I had already signed schoolboy forms. I don't think they would have approved.

Being a school that produced boys for the middle-class professions, academic standards were high and when it came to me leaving at 15 – an early age for such a school which expected you to stay until you were 18 – there was some resistance. Mr Bagley, the head, wanted me to delay my football apprenticeship for at least another year so that I could get a handful of GCE O Levels, as they were then, so that if all else failed at Ayresome Park I had something worthwhile to fall back on. It was an honourable sentiment and he only relented when Harold Shepherdson, assistant manager to

Stan Anderson at Middlesbrough and a prominent face on the England bench in 1966 and beyond, went to see him and reached a compromise. Shepherdson told my headmaster it was his role in life to nurture a pupil towards a job and this he had done. Mr Bagley did not give in easily and in the end it was decided that I should leave school and join Middlesbrough as long as I studied for some exams in the evenings after training and on day release.

I only ever wanted to play football and would have agreed to anything just to get started. For a few weeks as an apprentice I did as I was told but it was never going to happen and before very long I gave it all up, my schooling was over and with nothing in the way of qualifications to show for it. I was besotted with the idea of becoming a professional footballer and hadn't a clue as to what I might have done if Middlesbrough had kicked me out at 18, as they did to most of my contemporaries.

I nearly got into the England Schools side. As a 14-year-old in July 1969 I went for trials at Newcastle, billed on the letter I still possess as an instructional course for ESFA schoolboys, but my physique almost certainly let me down since I was far smaller than some of the big lads I met that day. Being left-footed they put me on the wing and of course my lack of pace and size counted against me and I got no further. My position, the old inside-left, was allocated to a lad named Gordon Cattrell, far bigger than me and almost adult-looking. Leeds snapped him up but as so often happens to outstanding, prematurely big schoolboys he never quite made the top grade although he did make more than 100 appearances for Darlington in the mid-1970s. Jimmy Morrow, the England Schools manager, came from Durham and I knew him before embarking on the trials but insider knowledge didn't do me any favours.

For all the liberties I took, leading a double life as a Middlesbrough would-be footballer, I have much to thank the grammar school for in terms of the good habits they insisted

I adopted. Mr Bagley and his staff believed in the virtues of diligence, respect for superiors and the pursuit of excellence. When I went training in the evenings at Ayresome Park I was getting much the same message from George Wardle so I found it a little easier to take on board his instructions than perhaps some of the other youngsters. At nine there was hardly anything of me in physical terms but George made sure I didn't get too battered and taught me how to look after myself without resorting to anything dubious or underhand. George and the school combined to make me the man I am today and the player I became. I had the ability, they moulded it.

Mr Bagley had only my interests at heart. He knew far better than I did that a life in football was extremely hazardous and was littered with casualties. The 'mortality' rate among post-school trainees is appallingly high even today with the academy system, which replaced apprenticeships, and which is designed to weed out at an early age those unlikely to step up. The financial rewards can be startlingly good for those who go on to become professionals but when I was a starry-eyed junior they were far more modest. The problem was that I was not bothered by the insecurity, seduced only by the wonder of playing football for a living.

George Wardle was convinced I stood a chance and so too was Harold Shepherdson. As England coach alongside Sir Alf Ramsey when England won the World Cup in 1966, he enjoyed a national profile so we felt almost privileged when he came to our little home to talk to my mum and dad about enrolling as an apprentice. I needed no convincing, even if it did mean leaving home and moving into the club's hostel not far from the football ground.

My headmaster would have preferred it if I had at some point switched my affections to rugby and gone into a 'safer' way of life but he acted in my interests always and I am now aware that he cared. And he did care because I have a letter from him which indicates his great satisfaction in my subsequent rise to prominence. The sad part of it is that the letter reached me only at the third attempt because of a mix-up over my address at the time and to my regret I never did get round to responding. I am not very good at answering letters, especially emotional ones like that from Mr Bagley who must have guided, cajoled and berated thousands of boys over his professional career. For that reason I'm touched that he took the trouble to track me down eventually and tell me how he felt about what I had managed to do with my life to that point.

Mr Bagley's heartfelt letter said, 'Those of us in school who know you have been delighted to hear of your success in the football world. I do not go to football any more but I follow your career through the columns of the *Sunday Express* and was very interested to read the half-page spread about you recently. You have certainly done extremely well to gain national honours so young and the school is proud of your achievement. We look forward to you soon gaining selection to the full national side and then we shall at least have your photograph to hang up in the school. All we have heard about you since you became a professional footballer has been to your credit.'

Full marks to my old headmaster for swallowing his pride and being dignified enough to offer his congratulations. I was no teenage rebel, no tearaway, and had never been a problem pupil. It was clear he desired the best for me. In return I gave football my best shot, always thinking in the back of my mind that he might have been judging my every move.

So there it was, one minute I was walking through the school gates, book-laden satchel on my shoulder, the next I was heading for Ayresome Park, to rub the same shoulder metaphorically against Harold Shepherdson and Dr Neil Phillips, also England's doctor, who had been important figures in that World Cup win four years previously.

It was a little hard to believe, but on Saturday 18 July 1970 as the rest of Durham celebrated the miners' gala day, known as the 'Big Meeting' in our area, I signed as an apprentice for Middlesbrough Football Club. I was 15 and a half and to that point it was the biggest day of my entire existence.

Two days later, as my school pals relaxed in their summer holidays, I was training. Old hands Jimmy Headridge and Jimmy Greenhalgh, long-serving trainers, barked at me and the rest of the intake, 'Get stripped and get cracking.' As the sun beat down on us I was tending the Ayresome Park pitch with a pitchfork, pathetically pleased to be there.

4

The Man For Stan

S TAN ANDERSON was the manager at Middlesbrough
when I said goodbye to my parents and headed for the
club's hostel, situated not much more than a goal-kick's
distance from Ayresome Park. But for the next three years
the most influential person in my life, away from the training
ground, was Nina Postgate, a formidable but kindly woman
who made our 'digs' her personal domain and became a second
mother to a bunch of teenagers all living away from home for
the first time.

My intake included Brian Taylor, Malcolm Smith, Alan
Parker, Peter Bickerdyke, Tony McAndrew and Bobby Hosker,
all of us proverbially starry-eyed, all of us believing we were
destined for stardom. Yet the odds were firmly against us
because the failure rate among apprentices was, and remains,
alarmingly high. The huge majority of apprentices never get as
far as being offered their first professional contract and while
there are famous examples of those who manage to bounce
back after being discarded at 18, the truth of the matter is
that most disappear without trace in football terms from the
moment they are told they are not going to be good enough to
play professionally.

The financial rewards for those who succeed at making the leap from humble, terrace-cleaning apprentice to regular first team player in the top divisions these days can be enough to set them up for life, but for those who fail there is nothing except the necessity to find a job outside the game and perhaps hope to play part-time for a few pounds extra. Managers say one of their worst jobs as the end of each season approaches is to tell apprentices on reaching the cut-off point of 18 that they are not going to be taken on. The dream is over and there are often tears as the manager attempts to soften the blow to tender young egos. It can be horribly hard. Fans don't always realise that for every player fortunate enough to put on an England shirt, the casualty rate among those who aspired to be professionals has been colossal. So it was with us that July in 1970. Statistically most of us were going to fail. But like soldiers going into battle, none of us believed we would be the ones to be struck by the bullet. Certainly I didn't. I had absolutely no doubts I would make the grade and I guess the others felt the same sublime sense of football immortality.

Mrs Postgate ran a strict boarding house. We had to be in the hostel by 10pm and no one was allowed out in the evenings at all after Wednesday as the weekend youth games approached. There must have been ten or 12 of us there at any one time, lads almost exclusively drawn from all over the North-East and now denied the home comforts we had taken for granted over the first 15 years of our lives. Some suffered from homesickness, some did not. I was in the latter category. While I loved my home in Durham, I was instantly happy in Mrs Postgate's care. Not that she made life easy for us.

We had to help with the cleaning, in particular in the kitchen which she insisted must always be gleaming when we left it. There was no alcohol and definitely no girls although it has to be said that at that stage of my life I was not interested in either. All I wanted to do was play football and the rest of life was unimportant and just got in the way. For all of this we were paid five pounds a week in our first year, six pounds in our second and seven pounds in our third. This was just about enough to buy a few essentials but no luxuries and yet I don't remember anyone complaining. To be paid even a meagre five pounds was just incredible because to be paid anything at all to play football was a bonus. We would probably have done it all for nothing just for the privilege of saying we were trainee professional footballers. It was a wonderful feeling.

Being away from home at such a young age helped my development as a person, of that there is also no question. Even in a controlled environment such as that at the hostel we had to grow up quickly and make decisions about our own lives. As I say, some adjusted to this and others did not but through it all I could see that there was not one among us who did not harbour a strong desire to succeed in our chosen profession.

Our citadel was the Ayresome Park stadium, now long forgotten of course and replaced by the Riverside, but to my generation it was a glorious palace of football. Only four years previously it had been a World Cup venue and the playing surface was every bit as pristine as Wembley's, a joy to play on. As one of English football's great amphitheatres, it was uplifting for Middlesbrough's players and intimidating for opponents and I was deeply sorry, like generations of our fans, when it disappeared. The pitch and the stadium was the pride and constant concern of Wilf Atkinson, our head groundsman, who treated it with the same love and care he would have lavished on his own home and garden. Wilf guarded the pitch as if it was his private property, almost resenting anyone actually having the temerity to play on it.

As apprentices, when we weren't training we were helping him tend his beloved turf, forking and re-seeding, repairing and mending, so that the playing surface resembled a lawn, particularly early in the season. Wilf taught us to have the same evident pride in our home pitch and we did. We came to share his enthusiasm and obsession and pitch preparation was never to me a grind or a duty. Of course, the North-East is not blessed with the best of weather and Wilf's job was made no easier by the rain, winter snow and heavy workload of a season's programme, which included reserve matches. When the weather was poor, the rain beating down and the players churning up the playing surface, fretting Wilf was on the pitch, pitchfork in hand, from the moment the referee blew the final whistle. During the week he wouldn't allow anyone to train on his sacred turf but the result of his diligence and devotion was a superb playing area and, as I came to realise later, it was as good as any in the country.

One of the highlights of our otherwise menial tasks was to tend to the dressing rooms on match day. The apprentices were divided and allocated to either the home or the away team and it was our job to cater for their every need. In January 1971 still fresh on the staff, I was delegated to the Manchester United dressing room when they visited Ayresome Park for an FA Cup third round replay and to that point it was just about the biggest day of my life. Those were the days when the United side contained such iconic figures as George Best, Bobby Charlton, Denis Law, Willie Morgan and Pat Crerand and it was wonderful just to be in the same room, listening to the banter and watching their preparations like a goggle-eyed schoolboy, which of course I had been a few months before. Best scored the only goal. By the time I got to play against Manchester United a few years later most of those had gone and World Cup-winner Stiles even became a Middlesbrough team-mate and an important figure in my early career.

For a few weeks I attempted to maintain my academic career at the behest of Mr Bagley but I knew from the outset it was never going to work and my three years at the hostel passed most happily. At the end of the week we would play our game

The Man For Stan

– all home matches were at our Hutton Road training ground – against the juniors of other league sides in the Northern Intermediate League and then I would depart for Durham and home for a few precious hours. If dad was not able to take me down to Middlesbrough before starting his own work on Monday mornings, he and mam saw me off on the Express bus back to Middlesbrough for another week learning to be a footballer.

However, not everything was straightforward. At 15 and small, slim and far from being the finished physical product, I was not always picked to play in the Middlesbrough youth team. George Wardle knew that exposure to bigger lads could ruin my confidence, not to say my health. We played our contemporaries from teams like Doncaster and Scunthorpe and, with due respect, they took no prisoners when they played the bigger clubs, as if they had something to prove. George could see the danger of exposing such a frail boy to the mercies of 18-year-olds and frequently in my first year left me out. My reaction was to cry, several times as it turned out, but I always made sure that if I was blubbing in my disappointment, it would never be in his presence. I didn't want George thinking I was a big baby, unable to cope with decisions which had ultimately been made in my own long-term interests. I was not fully grown until I was nearer 18 and by that age I had been promoted to the first team, well capable of looking after myself.

As a youth the big games were naturally against Newcastle and Sunderland and in the FA Youth Cup I achieved my ambition of playing at Roker Park, albeit in front of about 200 people, and at the dreaded St James' Park in the league. We also got to play on Wilf's Ayresome Park, remembering to replace the divots as we went. I think it is fair to say I acquitted myself well enough at youth level once I had grown a little stronger and crowds of any kind and size never got in the way of my performance.

In fact the only time I ever heard crowds was when I was playing for a team losing heavily – luckily only once or twice in my entire career – which is when you can hear every comment almost as if the perpetrator was standing alongside. All that ever mattered to me as a player of equable temperament was the state of the pitch, never the hostility of the crowd or the reputation of the opposition. I can't ever remember freezing on a pitch or being intimidated. Go out and entertain was a motto I embraced early on in my career. Having said that about myself, there were players who looked world-beaters on the training ground but who rarely did themselves justice in the heat of matches. Others rose to the occasion, whatever that might be, and among those was McAndrew, not the most skilful of youngsters but a fantastic worker and competitor and an example to any professional at whatever stage of their career.

Middlesbrough may have been a Second Division team but the presence of Shepherdson as assistant to Anderson and Dr Phillips, England's doctor in 1966, had brought a sort of international quality to the club and there was no doubt that we were underachieving in terms of first team results, something not put right until Jack Charlton came along a few years later. We should have been in the First Division because Middlesbrough was a big club with a big following but for some reason we were not and at 15 or 16 I didn't know why.

I looked at our first team squad and saw the likes of top scorer John Hickton, Hughie McIlmoyle, a striker exceptional in the air, goalscoring winger Derrick Downing, brave goalkeeper Willie Whigham, solid full-backs like Gordon Jones and Alex Smith and wondered why we were not better placed. Then there was the Irish winger Eric McMordie, a close friend of George Best and on his day almost as tricky and as whimsical. Add to them Joe Laidlaw and, later, Stiles and there was the basis of a team performing below the sum of its individual parts. They were all characters and as an impressionable junior you could only learn from them, good and bad. I fear the older pros took liberties with Stan and that was one of the reasons why we languished too long in mid-table when we should have been pushing more for promotion. We had the ability but not the organisation or collective desire.

Stan Anderson was something of a North-Eastern legend in that he had played for Sunderland, Newcastle and Middlesbrough and became the first to captain all three. The son of a miner from Horden, the record books say he made in excess of 400 appearances for Sunderland, 81 for Newcastle and a further 21 at Middlesbrough before replacing Raich Carter as manager at Ayresome Park, only the club's fifth since the Second World War, as his playing career wound down at the age of 32. He was described as a cultured wing-half in his heyday and was good enough to earn a couple of England caps when at Sunderland, going with the national side to but not appearing in the 1962 World Cup in Chile. Stan stayed with Middlesbrough until January 1973 before a surprise move to AEK Athens and subsequent spells at Queens Park Rangers, Doncaster and Bolton before retiring from football to care for his sick wife when only 48 in 1981.

Stan was an easy-going man who liked his players to enjoy themselves in training in the belief that a relaxed atmosphere would translate into a strong team spirit but it was not until Jack Charlton, the disciplinarian, came along that I realised how soft his regime had been. Stan was too familiar, too much of a friend to the senior professionals and in management that doesn't work. The great managers of my career, Jack Charlton and Lawrie McMenemy, knew there had to be a distance between themselves and the players without being aloof and unapproachable.

Stan had Shepherdson, coaches Ian MacFarlane, Jimmy Greenhalgh and Jimmy Headridge, the physio/trainer, in support and Wardle was an influence so that the backroom set-up was right but the results were far too inconsistent. To his credit, Stan loved the technical side of the game and it was clear how good a player he had been when the apprentices were commandeered to play head tennis. He would lead a team drawn from the coaching staff and the apprentices were made to play against them. The coaches didn't want to lose to a bunch of cheeky lads and it could become quite competitive, especially if it looked like we might win. Stan would shout at us, deliberately trying to put us off, not just to win but to teach us to concentrate and to avoid outside influences.

On the field of play, with a crowd apparently making all the noise, it is sometimes not appreciated by fans that the players are also shouting at each other, at the referee, the referee's assistant, the fourth official, anyone in hearing distance. It is easy therefore to lose concentration when there is so much information being flung at you. Stan made sure we learned that particular lesson and in my subsequent career it proved to be a valuable one. Let nothing put you off.

I still had some growing to do by the time I reached the reserves in the second year of my apprenticeship. Without anyone saying as much, I think the coaching staff began to see something a bit different in me at a time when they were beginning to work out who among my contemporaries was going to make the step up to professionalism and who wouldn't.

By now I was playing among grown men and those on the opposition were not inclined to take it easy against whippersnappers like me. Reserve team football these days has been watered down by the academy systems but when I was playing, the North Midlands League in the north and the Football Combination in the south had full programmes of 40 or more games and they were all regarded as important.

At Middlesbrough we had a core of players in the reserves made up of those on the fringe of the first team, those making their way as first- or second-year professionals and an apprentice or two like me. In my era there were players such as Malcolm Smith, Stan Webb, Alan Murray, Jimmy Platt, Pat Cuff, Brian Taylor, Basil Stonehouse, Mike Allen, Don Burluraux, Peter Martin and Steve Fenton. Among mature adults there was nowhere to hide and I had to adapt quickly to survive. Some of the tackles aimed at me would not have escaped red cards in these less tolerant times but defenders then could get away with some hideous challenges unpunished. It helped that I didn't react. Some players don't like the physical side to the game and it is their undoing eventually but if I got kicked – and I did – I was lucky enough never to let it bother me to the extent that I sought revenge and retribution. I also never moaned to referees, a fact for which I have the discipline of my schooling and George Wardle to thank.

At Middlesbrough the combative Graeme Souness would take care of any opposition transgressors and of course at Southampton there was no better an enforcer than hard man Jimmy Case. Jimmy wasn't a thug and never went in search of trouble but if it came, he looked after himself and those others around him less forceful or experienced.

Basil Stonehouse is not a footballer known to anyone except the anoraks of Boro devotees but he played an important part in my career for all the wrong reasons. Basil was a sound defender from North Yorkshire and a couple of years older than me. He was one of those who had come through the ranks, good enough to sign as a professional but in the end not quite good enough to get into our first team. I understand he later had a game or two for Halifax and then tried his luck in Australia. We were both living in the hostel at the time and Basil had decided for no obvious reason that he wanted to impose on someone the nickname Spike. I have no idea why. I was unlucky enough to be his chosen victim and the name Spike followed me around the country even as far as Southampton by the time I got there. People often wondered why I was known as Spike, coming up with all kinds of theories, but ultimately it was just the mischievous whim of a team-mate. Everyone knew me as Spike, except Bobby Robson.

There was a certain rivalry between those lads who had recently signed as professionals but were struggling to bridge the gap between youth, reserves and first team and the apprentices. Not unnaturally the 18- and 19-year-olds, as Basil Stonehouse would have been, saw us 16- and 17-year-olds as potential threats and we had to be put in our place. That is possibly why I became Spike. At the time I was being fast-tracked towards the first team and indeed made my debut at 17, in the process by-passing older players like Basil. I can only imagine what they must have been feeling. These lads may have been team-mates but they were also, in their way, your competitors even if Basil, for instance, and I didn't play in the same position.

There used to be a much-anticipated fixture every week between the apprentices and the young professionals at Shaw's Bowling Club and it often turned into a nasty little kicking match with all kinds of injuries inflicted and scores settled. To our shame these encounters took place on the manicured bowling greens and at the end we surveyed the damage we had done and retreated hastily, only to return to the same venue the following week.

There comes a time when decisions have to be made about the futures of young players. I was in the first team when my fate was decided and there was never any doubt that I was going to be offered a professional contract but for others the last year of the apprenticeship is a deeply worrying time. Some are clearly going to be good enough but for others, still growing physically and mentally, the outcome is less obvious. There was, I now realise but didn't see at the time, a sense of selfishness about us all. We were concerned only about ourselves. Yes, we were mates, living together in Mrs Postgate's tidy hostel five days a week but in the end all that mattered was getting a chance in the first team, possibly at another's expense.

Come the day and Parker, Bickerdyke and Hosker were among those called in by Shepherdson and probably the boss, who was by then Jack Charlton, and told the bad news. Shepherdson was acutely aware of the damage done to teenage psyches and, being a kindly soul, would make big efforts to find clubs for our rejects further down the scale. Others, who saw no future in football, were pointed towards other career opportunities.

Some borderline decisions have to be made, not everyone at 18 is an obvious success or failure. At Middlesbrough there was a big doubt about one Craig Johnston who was four or five years behind me in the system. Craig was a busy little tousle-haired midfield player who came to England from Australia, where he lived, as a 15-year-old after writing for a trial. His parents sold their home in New South Wales to fund his trip and Middlesbrough must have seemed a million miles away to a boy of that age. But he stuck it out, fighting his way into the Middlesbrough team before going on to join Liverpool where he enjoyed great success. At 18 his capacity for stardom was debatable. I know Jack Charlton didn't rate him but he was saved by George Wardle who saw in him personal qualities above and beyond those of an ordinary footballer. Jack took Wardle's advice and gave Johnston his first professional contract and he soon blossomed. But it was a close call. What might have happened had Johnston been fired we will never know but I suspect he would have returned to Australia, his gamble having failed. As it was, Johnston famously quit at 28 to go back and help his ailing sister, his last match being the 1988 FA Cup Final defeat by Wimbledon.

Later when I was playing for Southampton, a hard little midfield player called Paul Wiltshire was released at the completion of his apprenticeship, a decision which greatly surprised me. Southampton had an exceptional youth scheme at the time, they still do as the likes of Gareth Bale, Alex Oxlade-Chamberlain and Theo Walcott testify, and maybe Paul was just unlucky. But I felt there was something about him and I got in touch with John Neal, previously my manager at Middlesbrough and then in charge at Chelsea, and told him that he could be the next Souness. Paul went up to Chelsea, who were not the club they are now in terms of players and money, but sadly didn't get taken on. His career instead was spent in local non-league circles but he did take the trouble two or three years ago to thank me for trying on his behalf and I was pleased he had remembered.

I must only have played about 20 reserve team matches by the time I was chosen by Anderson for my first team debut. It all happened so quickly and I had no indication that it was about to take place. The date was 3 April 1972, the venue was Blackpool's Bloomfield Road and I was 17 years and 98 days old. Once more, Wardle was involved. The Easter programme was always hectic, much more so then, with three games taking place over four days prompting injuries, suspensions and loss of form. On Easter Saturday I played for the juniors and immediately afterwards Wardle told me to meet up with the first team the next day for the Easter Monday trip to Blackpool. I hadn't seen this coming at all so it was a bit of a shock.

We reached Blackpool on Sunday evening when it was revealed Hickton and Stiles were injured. I was to play as a conventional left-winger in a much-rearranged team. I roomed with David Mills, another North-Eastern lad who had come up through the youth team, but there was nothing he could do or say to reduce the nerves which made sleep impossible.

Blackpool were a good side in those days with Tony Green, Tom Hutchison and Micky Burns in their line-up, all high-calibre players, and of course Alan Suddick, the prize-giver of my childhood, was one of their more expensive signings. The pitch was bone-hard, the day far too hot for Easter and we lost 3-1. The late John Vincent scored our goal and the nerves never quite left me although I made a competent if inauspicious start. Burns later joined us at Middlesbrough and was kind enough to say I was the best player he had ever played with.

I remember sitting silently in the dressing room surrounded by all our top players, wondering if they would accept me, but I think they saw my potential and nursed me through my first tentative steps. Even so, for a youngster such a situation is always daunting and I feared making a crucial mistake. Fortunately I did not. The team that day was Platt, Craggs, Jones, Spraggon, Boam, Maddren, Laidlaw, McMordie, Mills, Armstrong and Vincent. Gordon Jones was our captain.

Stiles, an influential figure even while nearing the end of his distinguished career, returned to the side later and I kept my place for the following matches against Leyton Orient, Norwich and Preston. I was still a boy among men, earning six pounds a week as a second-year apprentice while my team-mates were earning anything up to £100 as seasoned professionals, not bad for 1972 when the average wage was not much more than half that figure.

While the others knocked back pints of beer after the games, I was still sipping orange and lemonade, trying not to look hopelessly out of place and juvenile. Some of the lads, perhaps as many as a quarter, liked a smoke, among them notably that fine Scottish goalkeeper Whigham, and it was not unusual for them to light up at half-time. Such an action would be unthinkable now but I guess management tended to believe that if a crafty fag aided concentration and made players happy then so be it.

There was also, on the Middlesbrough dressing room table, a bottle of brandy. I am told we were not alone in cultivating alcohol as a pre-match booster and that other clubs resorted to the same trick. Players indulged in a tot or two before going on to the pitch, but it settled nerves and got the adrenaline flowing and never did anyone any harm that I ever noticed. As a youngster, new to the adult world of pre-match drink and half-time cigarettes, it was all a bit of a surprise but I'm pleased to report I indulged in neither.

There isn't a club in the land now that doesn't have a long list of sports therapists, performance advisers and improvers, dietary specialists and you name it hovering around players with their stopwatches, clipboards and laptops. There seems to be as many of them at times as players and I wonder what they would have made of players smoking and knocking back brandy with the full consent of the management. It is a different game, or is it? Are we not complicating a simple sport? Certainly the England team is not any better than it was in 1966.

Nobby Stiles became something of a mentor in that first season and then the next. He may have been some way short of his Manchester United and England best but everyone liked him and warmed to him, based on the respect he deserved for his achievements. What stood out was a deep and basic will to win and I think we performed better as a team when he was in it, driving us on with his constant shouting and leading by committed example. I saw opponents who were frightened of him and his reputation and fled from confrontation. I liken him to Alan Ball, the same charisma, the same huge enthusiasm.

The following season I roomed with Nobby and it wasn't always a pleasant experience. Nobby bawled and hollered in his sleep, once causing me to wake believing we were being raided or something equally calamitous. Nobby wore contact lenses, most of his hair had long gone and he took his teeth out at night. Sat bolt upright in his bed, trying to come round from his nightmare, he was not a pretty sight.

There was always a sense of fun when Nobby was around, once cajoling Eric McMordie into throwing the cherished hat of experienced *Middlesbrough Gazette* reporter Cliff Mitchell out of a train window. I'm not sure Cliff, who covered the club's highs and lows over many years, saw the funny side.

In fairness, during my difficult and brief first campaign, Cliff gave me some good reports, some of which I have kept, and at the end of the season I could look back with some satisfaction at what I had managed to do. The record books say I was still looking for my first league goal having made five starts and a substitute appearance. We won ten of our first 15 matches but fell away after a mid-season slump and finished ninth, ten points adrift of a promotion place. I at least was on my way even if the team had still not got it right.

5

Another Shaggy Dog Story

A T THE first available opportunity I signed as a professional. I was just 17 at the start of January 1972 and would have signed on my birthday had it not been on Boxing Day, a few days before. Stan Anderson called me in to his office and I put pen to paper on a two-year contract which saw my wages shoot up from £6 a week to a basic 20. There was £25 for every first team appearance and bonuses which could, on a good week, take me up to £60. For every point gained I got £5 (in those days it was two points for a win) and there was another incentive which guaranteed a pound for every thousand fans over 21,000. In those days we were getting only about 13,000 to 14,000 at Ayresome Park so it was not exactly a generous gesture. Even so it was good money for a teenager from a humble background who was living the dream. I was actually getting paid for doing something I loved and never wanted or was qualified to do anything else.

The average wage now for a Championship player – the equivalent of the old Second Division – is somewhere between

£5,000 and £10,000 a week, and can be more if a player has a good agent. Later with Middlesbrough and Southampton I played 13 years in the First Division and on today's colossal, unfeasible money that should have been enough to set me up for life. I need never have worked again. But at the height of my career I never earned enough to save any for retirement. Am I envious? Of course, who wouldn't be? But it was a different time, a different place and there is no point in feeling jealous. I am aware of the money now swilling around in football and what it might have done for me but I don't think I would have changed the path of my career for any greater financial reward.

That path lay before me in January 1972 as a lad just starting to break into the first team. With up to £60 a week in my pocket I didn't know what to do with it all. Almost immediately I passed my driving test and bought my first car, a Volkswagen Beetle from team-mate Malcolm Smith, and the freedom that gave me enabled me to say goodbye to Mrs Postgate's hostel and move back home to my mam and dad's in Durham.

Leaving the hostel was a sort of rite of passage, a measure of graduating to adulthood and based in Durham I was home from training in time to pick up mam from the school where she worked and build a social life among the mates I had left behind almost three years before. I played badminton with George Wardle, watched by Jackie Milburn, Len Shackleton and, believe it or not, Neil Warnock and could have gone mad with the money now at my disposal.

Later I bought my father a car to thank him for all his support over my formative years and settled a few non-financial debts, rewarding those who had previously gone out of their way to help me. The car enabled my parents to get to our home matches in comfort and to contemplate stretching their horizons to watch me in a few away fixtures. Mam and dad were always supportive like that. When I was a boy they would watch me play for school, district and county in the morning and then go off to see John or Joseph play for their respective teams in the afternoon. We all appreciated their sacrifice.

Around that time, crowd violence at football matches was endemic and widespread and affected all strata of the British professional game for several disruptive years until greater measures of control were put in place like all-seater stadia and segregation. I used to worry about the safety of my family as they travelled to unfamiliar cities and was always much relieved when the tickets I had set aside for them had been collected. That way I knew they had arrived and were in place.

In 1972/73 Middlesbrough finished a creditable fourth, or so it would appear on paper, but actually we didn't do ourselves justice again. For a big club, we underperformed and lost our manager along the way. Yet Stan Anderson's sudden resignation in mid-season to manage AEK Athens led to Jack Charlton's arrival and some of the most interesting years of my life. Before he left Anderson brought in Alan Foggon, a former Newcastle player, from Cardiff for £10,000 and in the following month signed an ambitious but hard-to-handle Graeme Souness from Tottenham for another £32,000. It was Stan's last signing for the club, having beaten Spurs down from the original asking price of £35,000. Souness's debut against Fulham was also Stan's last game as boss.

Hickton was our top scorer with 15 and in the league we only used 21 players. Those who played most often were Platt, Craggs, Spraggon, Stiles, Boam, Maddren, McMordie, Gates, Mills, Hickton, Armstrong, Souness and Foggon. Stiles was captain, taking over from long-serving Gordon Jones who moved to Darlington in February after losing his place.

We made a poor start to the season, recovered to reach fifth by the end of November and then slumped again. The FA Cup defeat by Plymouth probably convinced Stan it was time to take the AEK Athens vacancy he had been first alerted about by the Liverpool secretary Peter Robinson who had asked him if he knew anyone who might be interested in it. We picked up when Shepherdson took over as a caretaker for a third time, losing only three times in 16 matches and winning all our last four. Even so, we were 14 points behind runners-up QPR at the end and in early May Charlton, who had been secretly watching us and weighing up our potential, was appointed.

My own contribution was that which might be expected from a teenager who had a lot to learn. The enthusiasm was there but not the stealth and the knowledge which comes with experience. I made 19 starts and scored my first – and that season my only – goal. It came at Villa Park on 28 October in a 1-1 draw and I have to be honest about this and say I don't remember anything about it. It was the first of 120 in the league spread over my career and of course it should be embedded in the memory, re-told to friends at every opportunity, but it's not. I don't know why. I could bluff my way through this omission by looking up the details but all I can say is that it must have been a fluke.

Souness proved to be an outstanding signing for Middlesbrough although there was always a provincial suspicion about someone arriving from a London club. At 19 he was bristling with determination to make up for what he perceived as lost time at Spurs where he had been unable to break into the first team. Alan Keen, later to become an MP, had scouted him for us. There was an on-field arrogance about Souness, which did not always endear him to opponents, but it was possible to see straight away that there was great potential and moving north nearer his native Edinburgh did him the world of good. Such was his ferocious desire to succeed that he had a habit when he first arrived of holding on to the ball too long and trying to win the game on his own. It took him time to realise he had to change and become part of a team. In fairness, he did. But when he first came to us we used to say sarcastically, 'Give Graeme the ball and we'll play with another.'

Joe Laidlaw left us before the 1972/73 season started for a stint at Carlisle and our paths didn't cross again until many years later when we found ourselves on either side of a great divide. I was playing for Southampton and he had been playing in midfield for our deadly rivals, Portsmouth, although he was no longer on their books. We were not in touch. One day our beloved old English sheepdog, Jevvy, went missing. We were heartbroken and had no idea how he could have disappeared. After all, a dog of his size and breed is not easy to lose, but he was well and truly gone. In desperation I got in touch with the local paper, the *Southern Daily Echo*, to make an appeal for his safe return, offering a reward. Surely someone must have seen him.

Soon afterwards on a Saturday morning as I prepared to play against Tottenham at The Dell, a big match by any standards, I got a call from Southampton Football Club to say a Mr Laidlaw has your dog and wants to meet you at Portsmouth's Fratton Park. So a few hours before a match at Southampton, I was standing outside the home of Portsmouth to talk to a man about a dog. Sure enough it was the same Joe Laidlaw and the dog was definitely Jevvy. Joe explained how he had been in a pub when a man offered the dog to him. Joe said he wanted £120 for Jevvy and after some brief bartering I gave him £60 and escaped from Fratton Park as quickly as I could. I don't suppose I'll ever know what really happened.

Jack Charlton was, like his famous brother Bobby and his uncle Jackie Milburn, very much a man of the North-East even if, again like Bobby, his playing career was spent outside the area. While Bobby will always be identified with Manchester United, in playing terms Jack was a crucial part of Leeds' rise to prominence under Don Revie and a ten-year, not-always-popular dominance of the First Division in the 1960s and

1970s. Jack spent 21 years with Leeds and joined us on his 38th birthday, an extensive playing career ended after 629 league appearances and 35 England caps. We had it on good authority that Jack was being lined up to come in as the long-term replacement for Anderson way before it was announced. Shepherdson was just keeping the seat warm until Jack finished his Leeds contract.

In many ways Middlesbrough suited Jack. We were not far from Leeds, enjoyed a big and vocal support when doing well and, perhaps most importantly, had the nucleus of a solid squad and team spirit which was reminiscent of Leeds in the early days when they went years without appearing to tamper with the basic line-up. Jack scouted us without a doubt and I think he saw in me a home-produced teenager who could hold down the left-side positions for years to come. I like to think also that Shepherdson would have marked his card as to my potential.

Just before Jack came to the club I had embarked on my run of 305 consecutive league appearances and 358 in all competitions. On 24 March 1973 against Aston Villa at Ayresome Park, a 1-1 draw, I began a sequence which did not end until August 1980. In many ways this durability, this capacity to play every game for years on end was what I became best known for. I thought nothing of it at the time and it never once occurred to me to step down all the while I wasn't injured. Squad rotation would have been regarded as laughable in the 1970s when managers simply picked their best teams and would never have rested their top men. It was all in place for Jack, the perfect job for him. Meanwhile we, as a capable set of players, needed his discipline and his knowledge of what it took to win matches.

One of his first, typically unpredictable, actions was to send me and Bobby Hosker, not yet released, to Jack's parents' farm at Leyburn for a week to fatten us up like pigs being made ready for market. Hard to believe now, but I was slim and slight, and little Bobby was much the same. Jack told his parents to make sure we got big breakfasts and evening meals and to be certain we worked on the farm doing all the heavy manual jobs to build us up. 'David,' he said. 'You've got to start putting on weight.' The problem is that he hasn't told me to stop.

The Middlesbrough players, mindful of Charlton's arrival, didn't waste the two-month summer break. Most had a quick holiday and were back in for light training, a few runs and five-a-sides, before the official date when we were required to start again but in the long run it paid off because we were certainly as fit as the new manager wanted us to be.

Jack was everything we expected him to be. He was an imposing sort of man, taller and more aggressive than his brother, and he brought with him much of the ultra-professional approach that Revie had inspired at Leeds. Revie had engineered something of a Leeds versus the rest of the world attitude at Elland Road and Jack was keen for some of that to find its way into the dressing room at Ayresome Park.

From the moment we met him for a pre-season tour of Scotland we knew his regime was going to be very different and a lot less fun than easy-going Stan's. Training was tougher, more structured, much less amiable and the match preparation was detailed and specific in a way that would have been foreign to us. But none of us minded. We wanted to be good, we wanted to play in the First Division and Jack's way was going to be the best. He was, after all, a World Cup-winner.

Away from the training ground he developed a reputation for not being the quickest to put his hand in his pocket. He cadged cigarettes, was the last to buy a round of drinks and was both tight with his money and cagey, but in some ways it endeared him to us. Jack had a funny way with words, occasionally inventing one or two of his own. We were playing Derby and Jack was warning an assembly of players about the dangers of their striker Roger Davies who had scored five the previous weekend and was an obvious threat. 'We have to be real astic,' he kept saying. One or two players started sniggering behind their hands, among them Maddren and Souness. Eventually, like a teacher interrupted by pesky kids, Charlton asked what was so amusing. Maddren responded, 'We just think you're stretching things too far.' We all laughed, Jack didn't.

Jack was no fan of directors and kept out of the boardroom as much as he could. Maybe it was because he didn't like authority, more likely it was because he didn't feel directors had any real knowledge of the game. Dr Phillips was the go-between, but it mattered little because Jack was an instant success, winning the Second Division title in 1973/74, his first incredible year in management. He was wise enough not to tinker with the squad he inherited, using the close season to make one vastly important signing. Nobby Stiles returned to Lancashire, sold for £20,000 to Jack's brother Bobby at Preston but his replacement proved to be an inspired piece of business by Jack. Bobby Murdoch came from Celtic on a free transfer.

Nudging 29, to the outside world it must have looked like he was winding down his career, but that was far from the case as it turned out. Bobby's reputation was huge in Scotland as one of Celtic's Lisbon Lions who famously won the European Cup in 1967 by beating the favourites Inter Milan. Boro fans must have thought he was coming south for one last pay day but they very quickly realised what a good player he remained.

Bobby was a little overweight and not the most mobile but he more than made up for it with his experience, his expertise and his fantastic passing ability, short and long. Jack and Bobby would have come across each other in the 1960s in some of the Celtic-Leeds battles, which captured the imagination of supporters on both sides of the border, and there was evidently a mutual respect. Jack endorsed the view of Celtic's Jock Stein when he described him as 'the best passer I ever saw'. Jack also described me as 'my little gem'.

Bobby's presence in the team made a huge difference to me and to the whole team who were lifted by the extra dimension he brought to us. Bobby worked the right side of midfield and I worked the left with the young and improving Souness in between. At Second Division level it was a formidable unit and it was little wonder that we ran away with the title in spectacular fashion.

Every bit as important to us was Foggon, a striker with pace enough to trouble any defence if he got behind them and whose 20 goals was another important factor in helping us return to the First Division for the first time in 20 years. He had won the Fairs Cup with Newcastle so he knew about pressure. John Hickton may have been coming to the end of his career but as a traditional English centre-forward he was always a danger and thrived on the service we in midfield provided.

Jack was fortunate in that although there was a useful, young group of players making up the squad on the fringes like Peter Brine, Brian Taylor, Malcolm Smith and Pat Cuff, the main core rarely changed. I played every game, so too did Boam and Maddren. The remainder only missed a handful of matches between them through minor injuries as we swept through the division, losing only four of our 42 fixtures. A couple of those came after we had clinched promotion with weeks to spare.

The mainstays of the team were interesting characters among whom I was very much the junior. Jim Platt, the goalkeeper, was the quiet man of the dressing room but with a dry sense of humour. Jim had taken over from Willie Whigham, who had always looked after me when I was an apprentice, making sure I was keeping out of trouble but who did all the wrong things himself, smoking, drinking and once setting fire to his own house.

John Craggs was the right-back, big pals with David Mills, a defender who loved to get forward, being an exceptional crosser and striker of the ball. Frank Spraggon was left-back, Shepherdson's son-in-law, a steady performer who was a completely reliable defender.

The backbone of that exceptional team was provided by the central defenders Boam and Maddren. They formed a terrific barrier, both strong in the air and dangerous going forward for corners and not much got past them. Maddren was the more mobile, a great mickey-taker but unable to train regularly because of knee problems. Mills was sharp, quick, a great athlete and willing to run all day. Only his touch let him down at times otherwise he might have become a truly outstanding player and he didn't always make the best of his chances. Mills was mature enough to know his limitations and used to come back in the afternoons and practise his finishing. We at Middlesbrough knew what he could and could not do and a subsequent big-money move to West Bromwich didn't work out, I think, because he tried to complicate his basically simple game based on pace.

Foggon was another quiet lad who didn't like training but he had this incredible speed which made him such a lethal opponent. Then, of course, there was big John Hickton, as good a finisher as I have ever come across, a real powerhouse of a man and a great crowd idol. If you ever wanted anyone on the end of a cross into the penalty box it was John. Statistics show his worth to Middlesbrough. Only three players have scored more than his 192 league and cup goals spread over ten years and he was an example to us as apprentices for the way he also used to return in the afternoons to hone and perfect his skills. Whenever he goes back to the club for functions it's clear he is still idolised by a whole generation of supporters who had grown up to his goalscoring exploits which, incidentally, included ferociously-taken penalties.

Jack watched this team develop rapidly, describing myself and Murdoch as the best midfield players in the Second Division, which was a welcome personal boost, as we went on to take the title by storm. Once again the stats make awesome reading when I revisit them. We went a club record 22 matches unbeaten, chalked up 25 clean sheets, six of them successive in March and April as our prize neared, and lost only once at home, 2-0 in the first match of the season to Fulham. My own contribution was five goals against Bristol City, Luton, Crystal Palace, Oxford and Notts County plus another in the FA Cup at Grantham.

Attendances soared once our success gathered momentum and it became clear to our supporters that there was a strength about us which suggested we could sustain our bright start over the whole winter. Jack said we were the worst at giving the ball away but the best at getting it back, a comment which hints at a lack of sophistication but we made up for that with great fitness and a tireless work ethic built around a rugged defence. We learned to hunt in packs of four or five so that if we lost the ball, as Jack indicated we often did, we got it back again promptly.

Our record shows we did it very well but there was no magic formula. Jack merely made sure we were rock solid, in the way Revie's Leeds had been, and used the right players for the system we had evolved.

As I remember, the London press didn't like us on the whole because they could see in us the possibility of Leeds Mark II developing, the way in which we were crushing opponents, just as Leeds had done, by not allowing them to play. There was no way we were going to apologise for being successful but for all the goodwill directed at Jack we were not exactly welcomed to the First Division by scribes when the time came.

Mention of Boam reminds me how we used to share a joke at the height of battle to ease the tension. We would be waiting for a corner when I would say to him, 'Do you know the size of the crowd?' Bearing in mind our crowd bonuses we loved a full house. He would respond by saying he had counted them and we would be going home with an extra £3 in our pocket. That sort of thing happened quite often so not everything was deadly serious, even when we were playing Newcastle and Sunderland.

We started our glorious season with a 1-0 win at Portsmouth then lost at home to Fulham, the only defeat in 26 matches. We went top on 29 September after winning 2-0 at Bristol City where Murdoch and I were the scorers and stayed there for the rest of the season. Our only other defeats were 5-1 at Nottingham Forest on 2 February, a strange aberration that one, 3-2 at Cardiff and 2-1 at Bolton. We finally clinched promotion on 23 March with a 1-0 win at home to Oxford when I got the only goal.

Benny Fenton, the manager of Millwall, was quoted as saying before our game with them in October, 'Middlesbrough are a tough lot and if they dish it out we must not stand around and take it.'

Luton, also promoted, were the only team who could remotely put together a challenge and when on 30 March we won 1-0 at Kenilworth Road, David Mills's goal was enough to make sure we went up as champions. Jack Charlton would have liked us to have clinched the championship in front of our own fans and was a bit grudging in letting us do yet another tour of a pitch. He looked at me celebrating at the end of the Oxford game, a promotion-winner at 19, and said, 'Enjoy it because it does not happen every year. Enjoy it as much as you can, but be professional.'

Jack, incidentally, had a Bobby Robson-type inability to remember names or got them wrong. If he didn't remember to call me Spike he probably referred to me as Neil, which I wouldn't have been over the moon about.

So there we were, champions with a month to go and we visibly relaxed, losing a couple of games at Cardiff and Bolton we would probably have won had they mattered. We were no longer by then a tight, relentless unit but there was a mental tiredness which I suppose was inevitable and I think we tried to express ourselves a little more than we had been allowed to in the run-up to the title. Even so, we put four past Bobby Moore's Fulham, scored another four against West Bromwich and we finished the home season in front of a full house by scoring eight against Sheffield Wednesday. Souness got a hat-trick.

The highlight for me of an incredible year was getting that goal against Oxford. All my nearest and dearest were there to witness it, including my new girlfriend. Murdoch picked me out with a trademark astute pass and I shot in from the edge of the box. There were fantastic celebrations on and off the pitch and it was probably one of the finest moments of my entire life. Not long later we were doing the first of many laps of honour and experienced team-mates said much the same as Jack. 'Take it all in, it might not happen again.' And of course it didn't.

There were other great moments. Bobby Moore's Fulham debut on 19 March ended in that big win of ours but it was just a privilege to be on the same pitch as a man of his stature. Only eight years previously, as an impressionable 11-year-old I had watched him on television lift the World Cup and while I always aspired to that sort of level, it all seemed a long way off sat on the sofa at my uncle's farm at Okehampton on the edge of Dartmoor where he had a slaughterhouse.

The derby with Sunderland on 2 March, as fiercely-fought as ever, saw Bobby Kerr and Dennis Tueart sent off, failing to stop us winning 2-0. Bobby and I, as I mentioned, were firm friends. Bobby had been something of a hero even of mine, albeit as a Middlesbrough player, for what Sunderland had done in the FA Cup of 1973 but we were social mates from the time we used to meet at the Cock of the North club on the A1. My first wife Julie and his first wife Cath often used to get together as a foursome with Bobby and I, and we remained pals even after we both subsequently remarried.

Luton, too, was a glorious occasion. We partied on the bus home as champions with six matches left and if the Boro fans had had their way we would have done a lap around the pitch every match thereafter. Jack, of course, was having none of that nonsense.

The fall-out was simply bizarre in its way. Everywhere any of us went fans came up wanting to thank us for putting Middlesbrough back on the football map. The whole team was invited to the Fiesta nightclub and asked on to the stage to take the applause. All the little supporters' clubs dotted around the area demanded we came along to receive various accolades. We were overnight celebrities and it wasn't always easy to take it in. We were a bunch of lads mostly from the North-East, ordinary working-class boys for whom it was a bit overwhelming, almost embarrassing. In a funny sort of way I was glad when it died down.

The reward was a world tour later in the summer that took in Hong Kong, Bangkok, Tahiti, Australia, New Zealand, all places I knew nothing about and never expected to visit. It was my first time abroad and certainly made a huge change from the normal team breaks in Scarborough. Jack had the added pleasure of being Manager of the Season and £1,000 better off, beating his brother Bobby in the last game of a superb season, 4-2 at Deepdale. Preston were relegated.

As a verdict, Jack had taken over a group that contained some very good players, many of them way better than Second Division standard, and moulded on them the Leeds methodology of unity of purpose, strength in togetherness and a willingness to run all day allied to high calibre skill. Jack knew what to do and did it with great efficiency.

It is not easy to single out any one player because we all contributed. We had a great goalkeeper, a strong and well-balanced back four, a midfield of contrasts and three players up front who could always score goals. A simple formula, and it worked from day one at Portsmouth.

We all felt, once the adulation had died, that we were strong enough to do more than just survive in the First Division. The test now for Jack was in improving us without destroying the very qualities which had got us promoted in the first place. While we toured the world in luxury we knew there were some big tests ahead.

6

Cautious Jack Cost Us

JOHN HICKTON had been a magnificent player for Middlesbrough over the years but it was clear that he was coming to the end of his career by the time we entered the First Division. No one had done more than John in getting us there but football is a ruthless game and to be perfectly honest he needed to be replaced if we were to make any kind of prolonged impact in the top flight.

Jack Charlton was not a sentimental man but he was as cautious with the club's money as he was with his own and kept his hand in his pocket throughout the summer when other teams were strengthening. It was always said, and I don't know if it's true, that Jack was on a percentage of the profits, which may have accounted for his reluctance to invest.

To the rest of the squad and to pundits outside the club we needed to go into the First Division with a new centre-forward, a new leader of the attack. That was no disrespect to big John. He had done his job in helping us to get that far and now we needed to replace him. The rest of the squad going into 1974/75 stood comparison with most of our rivals, even clubs like Arsenal and Leeds, but we were one player short of being serious contenders for all the major honours. These days teams promoted to the Premier League tend to regard staying in the division as a major achievement upon promotion but in the 1970s elevated teams tended to be more ambitious when they went up.

We had a very good team but we didn't have a younger centre-forward who would consistently trouble the best defences. Jack did make an inquiry for David Cross, a prolific-scoring striker in the mould we required but, canny as ever with his cash, decided not to pursue his interest when he learned of the sort of fee being demanded. Cross scored goals wherever he went, well over 200 in nearly 600 matches over a long career eventually, but at the time he was playing for Coventry and attracting plenty of attention.

West Bromwich didn't hesitate as we had done and bought him a year or two later and at West Ham he enjoyed his best years further down the line. Cross was tall, exceptional in the air but also a top rate target man, and would have been ideal, but it simply never happened.

In retrospect our failure to buy one more player was a mistake, but on such decisions are fates decided, and so it was with us.

Jack figured there was one more year in Hickton and the rest of the team was capable enough of looking after itself. On that point we were agreed. We went into the First Division fearing no other and it's true there were no obvious weaknesses spread over the rest of our best line-up. Souness, Mills and Maddren, for instance, were now approaching their prime and I wasn't far behind. Providing we stayed clear of injuries we could be a real force.

Brian Clough's Nottingham Forest were a year or two behind us in development and in coming into the First Division and I believe that if we had invested regularly as Clough did, we could have had similar domestic and international success. Clough had his own distinctive, possibly unique methods in getting the best out of his players and was never scared to make changes when he felt fresh blood was needed.

Perhaps we were too insular, too frightened of shifting players in and out. Our great strength was this terrific team bond, a camaraderie and warmth that would probably not have been matched anywhere else in the division. Jack encouraged this belief in one another because it had worked so brilliantly the season before in getting us promotion. But now we were in a bigger, better and far tougher league and it probably required one or two bold decisions.

That bond, incidentally, remains to this day through the Ex-Players' Association. Alan Peacock has been a prime mover in the organisation, as have Gordon Jones and Jim Platt. We had a big reunion in 2011 and Peter Brine came over from Australia to attend. The sadness is that of the team promoted in 1974, Maddren and Murdoch are now dead but for the rest of us the association remains a way of keeping in touch and rekindling that tremendous spirit of the times.

I suppose finishing seventh in the First Division in 1974/75 should be regarded as a success and in its way it was. We also reached the quarter-finals in the FA Cup and League Cup so there was much to admire but there was a lingering feeling that it could have been better.

The strength was once again our unity and our resilience. We bought no one until March when Terry Cooper arrived from Leeds and relied once more on the durability of our small, intensely-bound squad and we were lucky in escaping those long-term injuries we feared might undermine us. Jack used only 21 players and myself, Platt, Boam and Maddren were ever-present.

At least six others missed only two or three games and Hickton did as well as could be expected with eight league goals in 39 games, not bad by today's standards but another eight or ten goals might have made a huge difference. I am in no way blaming John and he never let us down in his wholehearted way but a top-class younger man could have spearheaded us into European competition and even the league title. We had the chance to strengthen by buying and didn't take it.

Eric McMordie was the only close season casualty, sold to York for £7,000, and in truth Jack never liked him as a player. Eric had plenty of skill but Jack saw in him other, less attractive traits and Cooper only came in for the last nine games of the season to replace Spraggon.

Frank knew his limitations and at £50,000 Cooper brought with him vast international and top flight experience. He was jovial and talkative and recognised he had come to a good club, well run, and a team laden with capable, largely unsung, players. Soon after signing Cooper, in only his third game, was sent off at Chelsea for remarks made to a linesman. Disbelieving his punishment, Cooper said, 'I thought the referee was pointing out a plane to me flying overhead.'

At that point, 22 March, we were third and stood a very good chance of winning the league. Way back in August, Jack had warned us publicly that he would fine us if we broke the strict disciplinary code (most of which was common sense) he had imposed and I'm not sure where plane-spotting appeared in his list of dos and don'ts but Cooper's dismissal coincided with an alarming and costly decline whereby we collected only seven points from our last seven matches.

The margin between success and failure was minimal because we finished only five points behind the champions, Dave Mackay's Derby, and three points behind Liverpool, the runners-up. Had we maintained our fine form of the first seven or eight months over those last seven games, three of which we lost, who knows what we might have achieved. It was our highest finish since 1951 but there were regrets, certainly by me, at the failure to sustain a challenge because it looked for so long that we could even win the league championship, which would have been incredible.

Disappointingly this year was our best ever and while we settled comfortably into mid-table for the rest of my time with Middlesbrough, we never again got into a position where winning the competition was a possibility. In my view this was a great opportunity wasted and bearing in mind the dominance now of a handful of super-rich clubs in the Premier League, such a chance might never come round again for Middlesbrough and clubs of their economic size.

We started well enough, beating Birmingham 2-0 away but then losing immediately at home in our next match in front of 28,000 to Carlisle was an unexpected setback and one of those results which with the benefit of hindsight was to count heavily against us at the final reckoning. We did, however, show the football world of what we were capable by beating Derby at their Baseball Ground, 3-2 in October, partly due to a fluke shot by Mills, as we were sure it was intended as a cross which deceived the goalkeeper Colin Boulton. We came within a few minutes also of beating Derby at home but were denied by a late equaliser, a quality finish from Kevin Hector.

There were highs and lows but the oddest result from our point of view was a 4-4 at home to Coventry in October just as we were beginning to find our feet. It provoked a bit of an inquest because we were not used to leaking four in a game. We prided ourselves on our defensive strength and to let in four was almost a sackable offence.

Overall I think it's fair to say we acclimatised quickly to the new division although it was evident from the start that every team had four or five top quality players and it was hard to spot weak areas to exploit as easily as we had done in the old Second Division.

Jack's insistence on a sound defence as a priority meant that the opposition had to find something extra special to break us down. Coventry apart, I think our only other aberration was in losing 3-0 at West Ham. I don't believe, as some people have supposed, that we were underrated or underestimated by the big clubs we now clashed with. In simple terms we had excellent players and a team ethic second-to-none and I know how much I personally relished playing against the likes of Billy Bremner, Colin Bell and Ian Callaghan.

They set standards to which I knew I had to rise every week and daunting though that was, I can't ever remember feeling at any stage that I was in any way out of my depth. I think Jack was delighted to be back in the big time after his single year out of it. After playing most of his career in the First Division with controversial, but often successful, Leeds and also with England, it must have been a shock to his system to drop into the Second Division and it was soon clear he felt he was back where he belonged.

Manchester United had suffered the humiliation of relegation the previous year but we met them in the League Cup quarter-final in December and Jack hit the headlines with an outburst against the referee Peter Reeves for what he perceived to be bias and asked for a replacement for the replay at Old Trafford. It didn't do us any good as we lost 3-0.

Ken Furphy, the Sheffield United manager, voiced his concerns about our tactics after his team had lost 1-0 to us at Ayresome Park on Boxing Day, my 20th birthday, which I celebrated by scoring the only goal. Lots of managers were secretly unhappy about the way we played but Furphy is reported as saying, 'I counted eight cases of shirt-pulling and nine deliberate trips on my players out there. Tony Currie was kicked five times and Len Badger had a broken nose.'

His comments didn't exactly provoke a row but there was evident unease among other clubs at our methods. We never employed strong-arm tactics but what some ruffled opponents didn't like was the way we stopped their flair players from expressing themselves. We smothered those who were likely to be the most creative, harried and chased them and wouldn't let them dictate. I am not going to apologise for that because it was up to them to counter our attempts to stifle, but in that respect I think we might have antagonised a few large reputations. I think we have to admit we were not especially liked or were especially popular beyond east Yorkshire but the record books show we were a handful of points from being champions, so we must have got something right.

From my point of view, just being able to run out at Anfield, Highbury, Elland Road and, yes, even St James' Park was a wonderful experience four or five years after leaving school. Mr Bagley's request for extra lessons was long forgotten but one lesson not forgotten were the words of George Wardle, which turned into something of a Middlesbrough mantra, along the lines of, 'Do your own job and half of someone else's.' It carried me through some difficult times and I know that Mills, Smith and Maddren were all better players for absorbing his philosophy.

Two of our toughest matches, to our own surprise, came against the combative, awkward opposition of non-league Wycombe Wanderers. We were fortunate to get a goalless draw at their place in the FA Cup third round, our customary efficiency disrupted by a sloping pitch, but they had no such advantage at Ayresome Park where my goal gave us a hard-earned and by no means pretty 1-0 win. There were long periods in both games when it was difficult to differentiate the First Division side from the part-timers. Wycombe eventually overcome, we beat Sunderland (I enjoyed that one) and Peterborough after a replay before succumbing 1-0 to Birmingham in the quarter-finals. So, all in all, not a bad first season in the First Division and it was so nearly even better.

Were we dull? We got 67 goals in the three competitions, so I don't think that was a fair criticism. Were we brutal? I don't think so either. We were hard-working, scared of nobody's reputation and we stuck firmly to what is now known as a game plan. We were well organised by Jack, knew each other's strengths and weaknesses and there were no egos or stars.

All of us had come up together from the lower division except late arrival Cooper and were determined to make the best of this glorious opportunity to play against the big teams. I was still very much a youngster, only 20 when the season ended, but some of my team-mates were not in the first flush of footballing youth and for them this was a late reward for career-consistency and a chance to prove a point or two.

Middlesbrough's success, albeit without actually winning anything, put one or two individuals in the spotlight. Souness, for instance, was called into the Scotland squad and England decided to have a look at me at Under-23 level. A year or two before that I had been called up for England youth trials at Lilleshall and since nothing came of those I was not especially optimistic about succeeding at the next step up.

I retain a letter, written in the formal language you would expect to receive from your bank manager telling you that you had exceeded your overdraft limit, to say I should report to Lilleshall. It is dated April 1973, Middlesbrough were in the Second Division and I was 18. The letter came from Denis Follows, secretary of the Football Association and under the headline Youth Team Trials, it read, 'I have pleasure in informing you that you have been selected to take part in the above get-together at Lilleshall. A detailed itinerary is enclosed herewith and I should be pleased if you will kindly complete the enclosed acknowledgement form and return it.'

Tony Waiters, the former Blackpool and England goalkeeper, was the coach and Eric Gates, albeit as an Ipswich player, was among a strong North-Eastern representation in a party of 26 which also included Barry Siddall and Joe Bolton from Sunderland, and Ray Hankin. Among other names who might jog a memory or two were Paul Bradshaw, Steve Powell, Mick Ferguson, Tony Morley, a winger who went on to play at full England level, and Steve Phillips.

I was already in the Middlesbrough first team, of course, and was experienced for a youth and, without meaning to sound presumptuous, would have been disappointed not to have been selected since I was already moving in a world which contained England stalwarts Shepherdson and Stiles.

In many ways the Lilleshall experience was a curious, slightly unsatisfactory one, a hotch-potch of trials, low-key practice matches, exercises, nothing in any way to suggest that we were the cream of the national crop. David Price of Arsenal and Derby's Powell got the nod over me in the midfield positions for which I was competing but in an odd sort of way it didn't bother me as much as it might have done.

As part of the learning process, of mixing with and finding out about players from other clubs it had its uses, but that was about it. Lilleshall in Shropshire was not the easiest place to reach in any case, but that was no excuse. It was the same for us all. But it was like being on a little holiday away from my Middlesbrough 'family' and was nothing even vaguely similar to a club atmosphere.

I say 'family' because that's what it was and in its way that was both a strength and weakness. The strength of being so familiar made us a very good team and the weakness was that it also might have made us a bit inward-looking and wary of the outside football world. I find it difficult to believe that I didn't get into the England youth team because I was from Middlesbrough, but there is always a suspicion that might have been a reason. Were we 'unfashionable'? It was a phrase used about us in some press reports and because we didn't have any big-name players I can see why we were called that. But all I can say is that when I was not picked to play for England's youth team I was genuinely not disturbed and was glad instead to get back to my 'family'.

Maybe I had grown up a bit by the time I was first selected for the England Under-23 team. There were no more trials, no pointless testing in unfamiliar territory. I was chosen for the first time in November 1974 on merit and because Middlesbrough were at that stage more than holding their own in the First Division. Having missed schools and youth internationals I began to think I was fated to go through my career without international acknowledgement so when I received a letter, less formal this time, telling me I was in the squad to play in Lisbon against Portugal I was ecstatic. To play at the top level in sport a player or performer must have a core sense of self-belief and I had that. I hope that doesn't sound arrogant but doubt can be a destructive force and I had always been comfortingly assured of my quality and prospects by the coaching staff at Middlesbrough. I was playing regularly in the First Division and I honestly felt I shouldn't be ignored any longer. I was ready and I was good enough.

Internationals are now played at Under-21 level and the concept of testing players two years older as a step towards full internationals has long been abandoned. I think this is as it should be. There are, of course, late developers but they will always emerge eventually. Most potential internationals should have been identified well before they reach 23 and 21 is about right. I am not in favour of holding players back and have always reckoned that anyone worth his salt should be appearing in league football at 18. I was still a month short of my 20th birthday when I was chosen for that Portugal match, which seemed to indicate that if there had been misgivings about me at 18, they had suddenly gone 18 or 19 months later.

Maybe this coincided with the appointment of Don Revie as the England manager in July 1974. Revie was born in Middlesbrough so there might have been some measure of empathy, I will never know of that, but he was aware of me when I came down to Leeds for trials as a kid and perhaps he had followed my progress with his home town club. Revie won half a dozen caps in the mid-1950s and the FA Cup as a Manchester City player and was once Footballer of the Year but his claim to fame was as manager of Leeds.

If you were a Leeds fan in the 1960s and 1970s Revie's management provided great days. They were an undeniably brilliant team with outstanding individuals in Bremner and Giles in midfield, the crunching tackles of Norman Hunter in defence, the powerful shooting of Peter Lorimer, and the sharpness in front of goal of Allan Clarke. But outside Elland Road they didn't make any friends.

There was a nastiness about them which made them hard to love. So it was something of a surprise when Revie became England manager after the ageing but more popular Joe Mercer had rejected the chance to make his caretaker position permanent.

The Leeds strength, apart from their obvious ability, was in their togetherness and this was what Revie stalwart Jack Charlton had brought with him to Middlesbrough and instilled in us. I think Jack would have put in a good word for me to Revie but I like to think he already knew what I could do and that's why I was in the Under-23 side at 19.

Revie didn't last and was gone by 1977 and that probably worked against me. He was trying to recreate his Leeds template with England, which with so many different clubs, philosophies and major personalities involved was never going to be easy and history tells us it didn't work. I have reason to believe he was grooming me for a left-sided midfield role because he was always encouraging me, always telling me at England get-togethers that he had plans for me. So it was a blow to me subsequently that he didn't translate into an international manager. With him went my hopes for an

England career because Bobby Robson evidently didn't share his opinion of me.

One such get-together of England players and potential England players took place at The Piccadilly in Manchester and I was one of those invited. It was a way of Revie assessing character so I didn't need telling I had to be on my best behaviour, not that I was ever the sort of person who went out boozing behind the manager's back. But some prominent players did. Tony Currie, Stan Bowles, Frank Worthington, Alan Hudson, all the flair players who, it could be argued, didn't play as often for England as they should. Revie had a suspicion of non-conformists since part of his success at Leeds had been based on a rigid team ethic that didn't allow room for mavericks, however talented.

What I liked about Revie was that he would send us thank-you letters after such gatherings and a little note of encouragement.

Harold Shepherdson's role as England assistant/trainer had been ended by Revie after 17 years and 169 internationals and he had been replaced by Les Cocker, his faithful sidekick at Leeds, but Cocker was equally well disposed towards me and I came away from that particular meeting in Manchester feeling I only had to keep being consistent.

The Under-23 clash with Portugal was no ordinary match since it was part of the European Championship and it's interesting now to look at the team and see that although there was plenty of ability and First Division experience, not many of us went on to play in a full England side and none had what might be called extensive careers at that level. The team in a 4-4-2 formation was Alan Stevenson (Burnley), Geoff Palmer (Wolves), Mick Lyons (Everton), Alan Dodd (Stoke), Alan Kennedy (Newcastle), Steve Perryman (Tottenham), Mike Buckley (Everton), myself, Peter Taylor (Crystal Palace), David Johnson and Trevor Whymark (both of Ipswich). Steve Powell of Derby replaced Buckley during our 3-2 win in front of only 3,000 Portuguese fans.

Gordon Banks was designated as our manager and the locals were not happy with the way Perryman, for one, wouldn't allow their ball players any room to express themselves and were delighted when he was sent off in the 55th minute. Kennedy scored an own goal but it was a superb win achieved on a day of intense, cloying heat and there wasn't one of us who didn't play a full part in a deserved victory.

I eagerly looked forward to further England exposure and it came two months later on 21 January 1975 at Wrexham in a friendly against Wales. Mervyn Day of West Ham was in goal, Steve Whitworth, a steady full-back at Leicester and the powerful Ipswich defender Kevin Beattie were named in the starting 11, as were Burnley's Ray Hankin and Ian Moores of Stoke in attack.

It was always hard for players and management alike to know what to make of such occasions. The players have come together from an assortment of directions, all of us anxious to make an impression and hoping to gel and show our best in a cohesive team unit, and those coaches on the sidelines unsure what conclusions to draw from a night at places such as Wrexham where the opposition was not so strong. We won 2-0 and while I did all that was required of me I still had this feeling that team-mates and management had it in mind that I was a winger. I spent my entire career, it seems, trying to convince important people I was not. As such it was not always easy for some of those from other clubs in the heat of a representative match to play to my strengths. Or so I felt.

I played for England Under-23s only twice more, my involvement at that step starting when I was 19 and finishing when I was still only 20. I will never know why it ended so abruptly because to my knowledge I never did anything wrong. Far from it, in fact. I was always told I had done well, carried out my orders and did the job I always tried to do with Middlesbrough so that I never had any inkling that I was not doing what they thought I should be.

In October 1975 we flew over to Czechoslovakia with the full international team for what amounted to a double-header. Peter Taylor scored our goal in a 1-1 draw at Trnava in a European Championship qualifier before we watched the seniors in action the next day. George Eastham, part of the England World Cup-winning squad of 1966, was the Under-23 team's manager. All the while Revie was making it clear I was in his plans and to keep working hard. Therefore it was no surprise to me when I was selected for the return match with Portugal at Selhurst Park on 18 November 1975. The team included Ray Wilkins and Trevor Francis and my club-mate Mills was among the substitutes.

Mills and Peter Taylor got the goals and we won 2-0 to book a passage into the quarter-finals. I was as sound as I could be without being outstanding and I looked forward in playing my part in the closing stages of the competition having played in three of the qualifiers. But that was it, all over. Banks had been replaced, which may have accounted for my absence as I search for excuses, but I was simply not chosen any more. It was almost another five years before I was 'rediscovered' and called into the B squad and then soon afterwards awarded my first cap in Australia.

No one ever said anything to me in the interim and I never asked. I just got on with my job at Middlesbrough and tried to put it out of my mind. Oddly, at the time of my Under-23 snub, I was neither hurt by my omission nor mystified. I didn't even regard it as a setback. My priority was Middlesbrough and the First Division and England had been a happy distraction when it came along. There was, curiously to some, no sense of loss to me until later when I started to become a serious contender for a full cap. By now I was playing 50 or more games a season and loving every minute and in addition, as if that wasn't enough football, I was coaching my brother's team, New Durham Workingmen's Club, and a Sunday side, Durham Boilers. These were lads I had grown up with and my feet were being kept firmly on the ground.

Would Brian Clough, another of Middlesbrough's own, have given me an international career? Clough was always the people's choice as England manager in the way Harry Redknapp was before Roy Hodgson got the job. Clough always appeared to have time for me and much later when I was awarded a testimonial by Middlesbrough, I got him to speak for me at a dinner in Durham. Unfortunately it coincided with that B international with Spain at nearby Roker Park and the FA had insisted I report to the team hotel on the night before the match, the night of my dinner.

Clough used his speech to berate me for not showing up at a dinner in my honour and then gave me another bollocking later. I should have been there, of course, with hindsight, but when you've waited almost five years, as I had, for another England chance you don't upset those in authority by not checking in when you should do. What made it worse was that players from Clough's Nottingham Forest, Viv Anderson and Garry Birtles, did not bother to report for England B duty until the following day.

7
Cup Glory And Failure

WHEN JACK Charlton did eventually get round to buying a centre-forward it was in December 1975 and he dug deep into the club's coffers to pay £72,000 for Phil Boersma from Liverpool, a striker of some pedigree who had been a fringe part of one of Liverpool's golden eras. As I say, Jack didn't spend anyone's money, his or the club's, lightly so this was a big investment by our standards.

What we had achieved in 1974/75, our first season back in the top division, had been remarkable considering that his only outlay had been on a left-back. But we needed to refresh some of the staff and to bolster what was already a decent squad, just requiring a player or two to make us serious contenders again. However, the Boersma signing proved to be little short of a disaster.

Phil was a nice enough lad, Merseyside born and bred and quick and lively on the pitch, when we could get him out on to it. At Liverpool he was behind Kevin Keegan and John Toshack in the pecking order but had made some useful contributions, often as a substitute as the Reds won the league title and the UEFA Cup. I think he had had a few differences of opinion with the Liverpool manager, Bob Paisley, and both had come to the conclusion that it was time for him to move on.

Mindful that he needed at least one new forward to supplement John Hickton, David Mills and Alan Foggon, Jack caused a bit of a stir on Teesside by breaking the club transfer fee record to bring Boersma to Ayresome Park. Jack justified it by saying that our new man could also play in midfield or wide so he had two or three players rolled into one. On that basis alone, his great versatility, and the experience of playing at a top class club, made his signing something of a coup and our fans were genuinely excited by the prospect of a Liverpool player coming to join us. We players were also pleased that Jack had splashed out for a well-known footballer whose record of 17 goals in 82 league matches for Liverpool pointed to his quality.

His signing also told the outside world that Middlesbrough meant business in that we were now signing household names, as Boersma was because Liverpool enjoyed such a high profile. Until his arrival our players had been home-developed or had been bought from teams like Mansfield in Stuart Boam's case or Cardiff in Foggon's. So Boersma carried a huge burden of expectancy among us all, and then spectacularly failed to produce.

Phil was super, super fit and yet never fit to play, there being a big difference between the two states. There was always something wrong with him and as a consequence his two years at Middlesbrough will not be remembered with any affection either by him or the club's baffled followers. In short, he was not half the player we thought he would be. Searching through the record books I see he played 47 times and got three goals which, even allowing for the fact that he didn't always play as an out-and-out striker, more often in midfield, says something of his struggles.

Jack must have wondered what he had done bringing Boersma across the country to the North-East. He was most unlike any player Jack would have encountered at Leeds or among those he had inherited at Middlesbrough. One of the qualities on which we based our success was durability, the capacity to shake off knocks and get on to the pitch much the same side every week. There were times when I went into matches not fully fit but it would never have occurred to me not to play and so it was with my team-mates. It was the Middlesbrough way. But poor old Phil never conformed to any of that. He was on the treatment table more than he was on the pitch and Jack became more and more exasperated.

There was one match at Old Trafford where Phil was a substitute and Jack told him at half-time to get ready to go on at the resumption. But Phil said, 'I can't go on now. I need 20 minutes to warm up.' Jack was open-mouthed. Never before had he heard such an excuse, if it was an excuse because I think he actually wanted to play. But not just at that moment.

We anticipated great things of Phil, perhaps too much, and he was not able to deliver, leaving Jack to rely yet again on Hickton and Mills for his goals while I chipped in with half a dozen that season. Phil moved on to Luton in 1977 and I reckon he must have been glad to get away. At least with us he forged a lasting friendship with Graeme Souness which was to stand him in good stead later. Phil became a qualified physiotherapist after his playing career wound down at Swansea and when Souness became a prominent manager at clubs like Southampton, Blackburn, Newcastle and Rangers, Phil followed him as a coach and as a physio.

The Boersma episode aside, Jack stuck to the players he knew. The failure of his star signing from Liverpool probably made him a little wary of entering the transfer market again and we went through 1975/76 with the same ever-reliable group among whom I was the only ever-present. And we did at least end the season with some silverware, albeit the Anglo-Scottish Cup which may not rank high among glamorous trophies but it was there to be won, and win it we did.

Not having been lucky enough to win the FA Cup or League Cup, despite near-misses, the Anglo-Scottish Cup will have to go down as some sort of consolation but it was fun while it lasted. We were placed in a group consisting of ourselves, Newcastle, Sunderland and Carlisle and the derby aspect gave it an extra edge so that the main aim was merely to make sure we didn't get beaten by them, and we were not. We beat Carlisle and Sunderland and drew at Newcastle, placing us in the quarter-finals where we were joined by Fulham, Mansfield and Blackburn and in Scotland by Ayr, Hearts, Motherwell and Aberdeen. The matches were played in September and we saw off Aberdeen in the next round over two legs and then Mansfield in the semis, again on aggregate.

Our opponents in the final were Fulham for whom Bobby Moore and Alan Mullery would have played in more illustrious competitions. There was only one goal scored over the two legs and I'm claiming it. One or two publications have it down as a Les Strong own goal but it was mine and I'm annoyed if posterity says it was his. My goal, I repeat, my goal enabled us to win the first leg at home and the second at Craven Cottage was goalless.

There was no open-topped bus through the streets of Middlesbrough but in its way it was an achievement, only won after nine arduous matches against good opposition, and it was another medal for the trophy cabinet, not bad for a lad just short of his 21st birthday.

There should have been a Wembley final that year as we were agonisingly close in the League Cup to glory. We played 59 league and cup matches that season and six of those were in the League Cup where we marched to the semis after beating Bury, Derby, Peterborough and Burnley.

The semi-final was a two-legged affair with Manchester City, the first at Ayresome Park. As now, Manchester City had some wonderful players but the difference was that the vast majority of City players in the mid-1970s were British. They were a great team to watch and much admired. They had at that time on their books Colin Bell, possibly the outstanding midfield player of his time, Rodney Marsh, Dennis Tueart, Mike Doyle and Peter Barnes, great players all. I said it was agonising and it really was.

We won the first leg in front of a big home crowd but only 1-0, which meant we had a huge task on our hands to hold on to our lead at Maine Road. One goal was probably not going to be enough. The scene was set for an immense second leg but Jack had every faith in this tight group of players and, as much to the point, we also had a strong belief in ourselves. Manchester City, a goal behind, were going to have to bombard us from the start and that was going to suit our counter-attacking style.

We needed the best of preparations and we didn't get it. The team bus was caught in traffic getting to the ground and as the minutes ticked by it was clear we were not going to reach our destination much before the evening kick-off. The order came for us to get changed on the coach because there would be no time to do so at the ground. We got there with nothing to spare for what was by that time one of the biggest nights of my life.

The match had barely got under way, and we were still finding our feet when I intercepted a back-pass intended for the goalkeeper Joe Corrigan. I beat him to it and shot against the post. We were inches away from a 2-0 aggregate lead and I'm convinced we would have gained confidence from that and gone on to earn a place at Wembley. We knew how to defend when it mattered. As it was, buttressed by their escape, City scored soon afterwards and with a huge and excited crowd behind them, they hammered us with a tidal wave of attacks and we simply caved in, losing 4-0 on the night. It was a terrible blow, no doubt about that, having got so close.

In the league we were again contenders but fell away badly. Ironically the start of our decline came early in March at Anfield where Boersma would have enjoyed beating his old club 2-0, but instead of taking heart from such an outstanding victory we failed to capitalise and fell away alarmingly. In fact we lost seven of our last nine matches to finish a distinctly moderate 13th and I think it should have been occurring to Jack that we couldn't go on using the rump of players who had seen us through good times and bad for so many years. There had to be changes. There had to be reinforcements.

But there weren't, not so you would notice them, anyway. For the season 1976/77 the stalwarts were still very much in place. Platt, Cooper, Craggs, Boam, Maddren, Souness, myself, Mills and Hickton had been together years and had done an excellent job in getting us promotion, winning the Anglo-Scottish Cup and stabilising us in the First Division. But we needed freshening, a charge of adrenaline that new signings bring to a squad. Phil Boersma was still with us, of course, and there were some good young players coming through like Stan Cummins, David Hodgson, Mark Proctor and Alan Willey but they were not ready yet to turn us into title contenders as we had been two years before. Hodgson and Proctor had not yet played in the first team.

In fact this was the beginning of the end for Jack Charlton as Middlesbrough manager. There was no way he should have been playing John Hickton, but Jack persisted. Hickton even started the season in the team, playing a few matches but his day was long past and it was wrong for Jack even to have thought he could lead the attack yet again through another long and arduous campaign, especially if it ran to 59 games as the last had done. Alan Foggon had gone, briefly to Manchester

United and then on to Sunderland two months later without playing a game for United. United are said to have lost £15,000 on the two deals.

The problem was we didn't replace Foggon, whose pace and goals had been so important to us. In retrospect it was the beginning of the break-up of Jack's solid backbone and we never quite recovered.

Murdoch was clearly finished and with Hickton now a spent force, Jack had to do something. His answer was to bring in Alf Wood on a free transfer from Hull City at the start of October. To say that Wood's signing was not quite what we had been looking for would be an understatement. Alf had started his career at Manchester City as a defender and on being converted to centre-forward had some lower division success at Shrewsbury, Millwall and Hull. Alf was a nice lad, a steady player, awkward to mark, I imagine, and he put himself about. But there was no way Alf was a First Division player. Other teams, noting his scoring prowess, would have looked at him over the years and realised he didn't have the pace, the class, the ingenuity to open up top defences. He battled hard enough but the Middlesbrough fans, who had been hoping for a big name or two, were understandably disappointed for us to be bringing in a player from our neighbours, and for nothing. Why Jack was not more ambitious or adventurous, I only wish I knew.

The problem was that with those three star players either gone or on the way out and not being adequately replaced, others became restless. Mills was placed on the transfer list in December briefly although he went on to get 18 goals and clubs started to look at Souness and myself. I was not aware of anyone actually bidding for me but there were always rumours, which can be flattering if big clubs are involved.

Jack's answer would surely have been that we weren't a bad side without Foggon, Hickton and Murdoch because on

9 October we beat Norwich 1-0 to go top of the First Division for the first time since 1950. Sadly we couldn't stay there. We did get back to fifth in February but we were never serious challengers because we lacked goals. While Mills got 18, 15 in the league, I got ten but Hickton didn't get on the scoresheet before being loaned to Hull and Alf Wood managed only two.

Mills was getting frustrated. I thought he was a great player and it was a surprise to me that no one came in for him when he went on the list that December. In fact it was almost another three years before he got away, to West Bromwich Albion for a British record £550,000, and he was never as effective away from Middlesbrough as he was with us. I am thankful he stayed since without him I'm not sure what might have happened because he was almost carrying the attack on his own for a time.

At one stage we went 12 matches without a win, prompting Jack to say we were on the crest of a slump. What did he do about it? Not a great deal. He still maintained great faith in those who had stayed loyal to him over the years, indeed myself, Craggs and Boam played in every game, but we ended in mid-table again (12th) and there was a disquieting lack of progress or purpose. It did cross my mind to follow Mills in asking to leave but we always had just enough good results to justify staying.

My friend Bobby Kerr provided some light relief when we went to Sunderland and were thrashed 4-0 in February, 1977. Bobby was playing against us and Sunderland were one up in no time and coasting through the second half. At one point it looked as if Sunderland might run up a cricket score so during a lull in play I told Bobby to ease up on us. Bobby said, 'I tell you what. I'm going to leave a gap for you and will chase you, but making sure I don't catch up with you.' Sure enough, he was as good as his word. A big opening appeared where he should have been which let me in with only Jim Montgomery, the goalkeeper, to beat but Monty made the save and the chance of a plotted consolation had gone. Bobby smiled as I went back towards the halfway line. 'You've had your chance,' he said, and I didn't get another.

We had some measure of success in the FA Cup after a shaky start at Wimbledon, then a non-league side, in the third round. Not so many years later Wimbledon, by then an established First Division side after a meteoric rise through the divisions, actually won the Cup but here in January 1977 they were still very much the underdogs. We were lucky to get away with a replay with Jack blaming the Plough Lane pitch, 'We couldn't play football today, the replay will show if Wimbledon can play.'

In fairness to Wimbledon the replay confirmed Jack's worst fears. They could play and were overcome only by my penalty. By now I was taking Middlesbrough's penalties and continued to do so throughout my career when required, although at Southampton there was always a queue in front of me. I used to practise spot kicks in training at Middlesbrough by telling Jim Platt, our goalkeeper, which corner of the net I intended to place my shots. The run-up had to be right but I scored many, many more than I missed.

I used to place them but my policy changed after having one saved by Everton's Neville Southall at The Dell when I was playing for Southampton. It was not uncommon for the Dell pitch to be extremely muddy and unpredictable and after we had been awarded a penalty, the spot was repainted by the groundsman while I waited and then I slipped as I ran up to take it. From then I resolved to blast my shots so that goalkeepers, as Gary Bailey of Manchester United once did, might guess right but they would be beaten for power.

We were beaten eventually 2-0 in the quarter-final at Liverpool but the round before we produced our best display of the season in beating Arsenal 4-1 at Ayresome Park. Souness was outstanding that day, dictating play from the middle of the pitch, and Mills caused havoc by scoring a hat-trick. We always enjoyed playing teams from the south at our ground. There were some, who might not have been the stereotypical southern softies, who seemed not to like coming so far north and rarely gave good accounts of themselves. We were always ready for them. But we were never able to sustain a run of good results so we fell away to 12th in the league and made no lasting impression in the cups.

All the good work of previous seasons was in danger of slipping away through managerial inertia. Maybe Jack had run out of ideas. He was certainly not seen at his best in the transfer market where, Murdoch apart, he had clearly failed to bring in the high class replacements we so desperately craved. On 21 April after a home defeat by QPR, he resigned, claiming he needed six months' rest to recharge his batteries. I can't say I was surprised, perhaps only by the timing because there were still five matches to be played and he might have seen the season out.

As it was, Harold Shepherdson came to the club's aid, as he had done so often in the past, and became caretaker yet again. It says much for Harold, a Boro man to his bones, that we improved instantly, going unbeaten over the last five matches in which I scored twice in a 3-0 home win over Manchester United. As Jack rested, Harold made it clear that he didn't want the job permanently so the hunt was on for a long-term successor.

I think Jack realised his chance had passed him by. He had lost his way. There was that huge opportunity for him to build a truly great side when we were promoted but he didn't take it. I think he lacked confidence and know-how in the transfer market having come from Leeds where the culture was rarely to recruit from outside. There is a saying in football that the time to sign players is when you are successful, not when you're struggling. Jack led a great group of players out of the First Division but didn't add to them. We can blame Boersma and Wood as much as we like in isolation, but that would be unfair because there should have been others before and after them, many more in fact.

Knowing when and whom to buy and when to sell is a key part of a manager's job and in that respect Jack could have learned some lessons from the other major manager in my career, Lawrie McMenemy, who was a master in the market. Jack didn't have that flair, which was a pity because we were so near to success but so far in the end. Jack could see the group of players who had worn the Middlesbrough colours with such distinction beginning to break up and it was time to go, providing an opportunity for the Middlesbrough board to be bold in their choice of Jack's replacement. Five days after the end of the season they appointed little-known John Neal and charged him with the task of doing what Jack had not done, refurbish an ageing squad.

Neal had awoken interest for what he had achieved at Wrexham, guiding them to the quarter-finals of the European Cup Winners' Cup in 1972 and the quarter-finals of the FA Cup but his arrival might have annoyed some supporters who had been expecting someone of a higher profile. Neal was from County Durham so he appreciated the mentality of the North-East but compared with Jack he was quiet, unassuming and not prone to acting without deep thought. Coming to Middlesbrough was a big step up for him but it was also a difficult one.

The club was about to go through a transitional stage and it was clear straight away that the older pros were going to test him out. A few days after his appointment we were booked for a tour of the Far East to include Hong Kong and then Australia. Souness and Boersma got as far as Hong Kong and when the rest of us flew on to Australia, stayed there in open defiance.

There was another time when Neal had to suspend Cooper for not going on another trip to Norway. Souness was a bit of a ringleader here and some of the more experienced players followed his example, Neal relying on me to some extent to keep the dressing room stable.

New players needed to be brought in and a fair few others needed to be shipped out. One of those inevitably was Souness who had been outstanding for us over the previous three or four years but was becoming stale. Neal had disciplined him in early January, suspending him for seven days and he never played for us again. On 11 January 1978 he was sold to Liverpool for £325,000, a transfer record between English clubs at the time, and it was a relief to all concerned, not least Neal whose authority was being questioned continually.

Souness, an excellent one- and two-touch footballer, needed to be among top players and firm management, as he would have encountered at Liverpool. He had got to the stage with us where he wouldn't release the ball, which upset the rest of us at times and the pleasant, easy-going Neal was reluctant to impose firm control on senior members. Although he brought in good players of his own like John Mahoney, a committed and terrier-like midfielder, for £90,000 from Stoke, and the too-nice Billy Ashcroft, a gentle giant of a centre-forward from Wrexham for a club record £135,000, they were not to be compared in terms of calibre with the likes of Souness.

I could see the drop in class and quality and for the first time I was becoming seriously unsettled. I liked Neal for the way he encouraged us to express ourselves and to be more expansive in a way that the rigid Jack would never have allowed. But there was talk of Tottenham and Leeds showing an interest in me and for the first time I began to think of a life beyond Ayresome Park. Neal thwarted that by making me the midfield playmaker where Souness had once patrolled aggressively, but there was no denying we had become a selling club and were not replacing the better players.

Cummins was in and out of the team around that time, once described as the first million pound player. Neal dropped him after one match to Stan's great dismay. 'You can't do that,' he said to the manager. '*The People* newspaper gave me marks of nine out of ten last week.' John had to explain to him that good marks arbitrarily handed out by a reporter under pressure were not necessarily a reliable guide.

One of Neal's first acts was to dispense with the under-achieving Boersma but we were poor that season, recovering from a dreadful start in which we won only one of our first eight matches to finish 14th. There was however a definite hint of a club going backwards.

I was the only ever-present that season as my long run of consecutive matches continued so that some fans began to think I could go on forever. But around that time I began to feel jaded and the supporters, who had stood loyally behind me from day one, suddenly started to turn against me, not in any great numbers but enough to make me realise that perhaps I should step aside for a bit. Passes were going astray, I became sluggish, slow to see situations developing and must have looked like a man going through the motions without enthusiasm or energy.

I went to see the manager to tell him I thought I was in a rut and to see what he thought might be for the best. Neal had come to depend on me as the Anderson/Charlton team began to break up because I got on with my job and didn't complain. He said, 'David, even on half capacity, no one could replace you. You will come through it.'

The problem was that since getting into the team at 17 I had also played for England Under-23s, England B, pre-season, post-season and other matches likes the occasional testimonial.

It all mounted up and while I loved playing everyone gets tired in their job sooner or later.

I was living at home at the time and at least I had the support of my parents during this blip in my career, or so I thought. I used to drive from Middlesbrough to Durham on Saturday evenings after games wondering where it was all going wrong. But instead of getting a sympathetic hearing from mam and dad all I got was an anxious and concerned inquisition. They had watched the matches, noted the crowd reaction and seen me struggling to cope where once I had been one of the club's best players. Then it happened a second Saturday and finally a third. The pressure was so great even at home and as they questioned me about my listless lack of form, I burst into uncontrollable tears. The only place I thought I was safe from this mounting criticism would have been the sanctuary of my home. But here I was sobbing my heart out on the kitchen table.

The trouble was my parents had become fans and they wanted answers as much as the next man on the terraces. Only then did they realise what they had done and start to get behind me, showing the sort of remorse and support expected of parents in a highly unusual situation. It was just that they couldn't separate being supporters from being parents.

I came through it eventually but it must have lasted half a season and the more I thought about it, the worse it became for a time. The problem lay in the fact that I had been a senior player, laden with responsibility from an early age and had been taken a little for granted. Not missing a game of any sort for eight years or so had taken its toll. I consoled myself that even at my lowest ebb no opponent ever overran me and I was never dire. I was just ineffective and plodding, anxious to get through the 90 minutes without making mistakes or being exposed. A crisis of confidence, I suppose. John Neal might have taken the heat off me by resting me but it showed the state of the club's playing resources that he had absolutely no intention of leaving me out and in any case had no one able to replace me.

Neal did occasionally flex his managerial muscles and not allow matters to drift, as he had done in my case. Just before Christmas 1978 we decided to have a players' party three days before the festive season and an important match with Chelsea. John got wind of it and was horrified. He called myself as a senior player and Jim Platt, our PFA representative, into his office and he told us he was going to fine us all if we partied, but we resolutely refused to back down. We told him we would not overdo the booze and could be trusted to behave responsibly.

A couple of days later, on 16 December, fully recovered from our night out, we beat Chelsea 7-2 with Micky Burns scoring four. John kept his thoughts to himself and didn't carry out his threat to hit our pockets. Instead we cheekily put forward a motion saying we thought we should have a party every week.

8

My Biggest Regrets

THE BIGGEST regret of my life is being estranged from Claire, the daughter from my first marriage. The second was marrying her mother, Julie. The breakdown of my relationship with Claire was something I fought desperately against but as I write, I'm not even sure if I shall see her again or my two grandchildren whom I have only ever met fleetingly. The only good to come from a long and bitter tale was that I met and married Maureen and we now have a happy and complete family together, but the hurt remains and is as deep as ever.

I suppose at the heart of it was my lack of knowledge of women, the outside world even, so that I was married at 21 and burdened with a mortgage at a time when most lads are out enjoying themselves. Before I met and married Julie White I had only one real girlfriend, Kathleen Brown, who I had met at a Belmont youth club. I may have been a First Division footballer but I was still living at home and was a bit naive. Unlike many of my contemporaries I had a nice car and plenty of money, so much in fact I didn't know what to do with it. Kathleen's parents, Wilson and Ruth, used to watch our games but they were not starry-eyed so when I asked if I could get engaged to their daughter, they said no because they felt Kathleen was too young. I don't blame them. I would have done the same but the result was that the relationship fizzled out and we drifted apart.

On the rebound I met Julie and things were never right almost from the very beginning. With a footballer's wages burning a hole in my pocket I bought a three-bedroom house off plan in Hett village as an investment from estate agent Mike Weston, the former England rugby international with whom I played cricket at Durham, and longed to settle into it.

Julie and I had only been going out about six months when she said she was pregnant, a shock at the time because that sort of thing was still frowned upon outside marriage. I did what I felt was honourable and asked her to marry me. Soon after we had announced our engagement she told me she had lost our baby but by then we were committed to a big wedding in Ferryhill. I think I knew I was making a mistake even on my wedding day in 1976 although three years later we had our lovely daughter together. I had hoped Claire would be the cement that would hold our relationship together but it didn't work out that way and I suppose it was unfair to expect a baby to be able to do that.

Almost from day one I felt trapped, smothered in part by Julie's parents. Every time I came home from training there they were, sitting around our smart new home, and I came to the conclusion that she had married me to have a baby for herself and her family. This made me resentful, so much so that I started not to want to go home, taking up golf to fill the afternoon hours when I might have been with my wife and baby. I remember parties with the Sunderland players and we had a good social life together but somehow it was not what I wanted.

One summer I had hoped we would go on holiday to St Lucia but Julie wanted to leave the baby at home and I was not having that so we didn't go. Little irritations became major clashing points, not least the way she chewed gum to conceal her smoking. I hated smoking and I quickly realised that I had got myself into a relationship I disliked almost as much, made tolerable only by the wonderful presence of our daughter. While Julie basked in the reflected glory of being a footballer's wife, I became tense and anxious and fearful of the future, a future that I knew could not possibly involve her.

I wasn't looking for another relationship, far from it, but it happened. I played golf with Bobby Kerr at Boldon. A friend of ours and a local businessman, Terry Simpson, invited us for lunch to meet some of his clients and it was then that we chanced upon Maureen and her best friend, Linda Kirtley. Three of us were married to other people and Linda was in a relationship, Maureen had two children and there was no suggestion of anything untoward going on between any of us. But we all found we liked each other's company and we used to meet regularly just to catch up and I suppose it gradually became clear the more we talked that none of us were in relationships that we liked.

I listened to Maureen and she listened to me and it was six months before we even so much as kissed. Even then I wondered why she appeared to want me. Maureen was three years older but being in her company only compounded the feeling that I had made the wrong choice. I went home one day and told my wife I was moving out and returning to live with mam and dad. It was not a decision taken lightly. No one likes to admit to a failure in marriage and more so in this case because I had worked particularly hard as a footballer to get where I was.

Julie's parents came over to my family home to sort it out and I fled upstairs and went to bed while below me I could hear a major row taking place between the two sets of parents. Julie's dad, a prominent mason incidentally, insisted

I went back to their daughter but dad said, 'He's staying with us.'

Having made my decision, which I knew was bound to be costly, although at that stage I didn't know how costly, Maureen later made hers to leave her husband. At the same time Bobby Kerr was getting together with Linda, deserting his family home to be with her, two prominent North-Eastern footballers breaking up their marriages at the same time. The two 'new' couples used to go to the Ramside Hall Hotel, a four-star luxury hotel and golf complex, on Saturday nights but any hope of discretion was ruined by me showing up in my sponsored car with my name emblazoned all over it.

Bobby and Linda eventually married. Maureen was especially brave in difficult times for us all. She had left her husband, Howard, and taken their two sons aged 11 and seven with her to rented accommodation in Washington, County Durham, and while I saw her every day I went home to mam.

As the relationship blossomed it became common knowledge and inevitably attracted interest. I took Maureen and her children to Scarborough for a weekend to get to know them all better and I became aware that my mother-in-law had gone to the *News of the World* and spilled the beans about how First Division footballer David Armstrong had abandoned his wife and daughter to run off with an older woman and her 'three' children. Good *News of the World* copy, except they got it wrong about the number of children. Even so, it terrified me, the thought of our affair becoming national news and on the day the article appeared I went down to the nearest newsagent and bought every copy of the paper in the shop.

In retrospect it was a daft thing to do and the only winner there was the newsagent but the bitterness had dug deep and we knew our love was going to be severely tested if it was to survive. And survive it did thanks to Maureen's love and resilience and our determination to make it a success.

This all coincided with my testimonial season at Middlesbrough, awarded to me at 26 which is especially young to receive such an accolade but recognition of my nearly ten years of service and for my loyalty in staying with the club when other major players were moving on. Now I was about to do the same. Feeling that I needed a fresh start away from the prying eyes and the gossip in the North-East I asked for a transfer, which must have felt to some as a betrayal. Then, with my emotions all over the place, I had to go through the messy business of a divorce.

Up to this point I was wealthy for a lad of my age and background. There was the house on which by now there would be a healthy profit if sold and of course money coming in from my testimonial, all the cash-raising social events plus a match from which I was entitled to the gate proceeds. When it came to the court hearing to work out who got what I was by now a Southampton player having moved about as far as possible from Middlesbrough, the little matter of 320 miles. I knew I would have to be prepared to pay Julie a considerable amount of money but I didn't want to be greedy because I wanted the best for my daughter.

Anxious to prevent my wife getting away with too much I bought myself a smart red Mercedes from Sparshatts garage in Hampshire and headed north again for the judgement. I had been advised to hire a barrister at Teesside Crown Court, which in itself cost a fortune, only to be confronted by a judge who was known by reputation to favour the women in divorce cases. To prove it the judge sported a bandage across his head, apparently the legacy of a chair thrown at him by a man who had been the victim of one of his damning verdicts. Now it was my turn.

The details of the marriage breakdown were read out and it became clear to the judge that I was heavily in the wrong. I had gleaned about £11,000 from my testimonial year and I didn't expect much of it to remain in my hands, and I was absolutely right. Adjusting his bandage, the judge said Julie could have the house and its contents, that I should finish the payments on a car I was buying for her and that I should pay £15,000 a year maintenance for Claire until such time as she completed her education or if Julie remarried. Claire was about three at the time. In addition I had to pay Julie's costs and my own. 'And you,' sneered the judge, 'can keep and live in your red Mercedes.'

It was a staggering blow. I had been made an example of, to use the judge's words and I came out of that court and burst pathetically into tears. I sobbed and sobbed. My lawyer advised me to appeal but I looked at him and said what with. I had no money any more. I am sure there were people thinking that as a top footballer I would be able to cope with the financial penalties but the money then was nothing like it is today.

Here I was, an England footballer, completely skint. My first contract at Southampton promised me £35,000 a year before tax. From that I had to pay the £15,000 maintenance and eventually a mortgage on our property at Fair Oak, which even now still has a few years to run. Julie only remarried when I stopped earning the comparatively big money from my playing career.

Being those 320 miles from the scene of the 'crime' was a great blessing but it was a huge upheaval for us all, not least Justin and Christian, Maureen's two boys. They had been taken from their home, from everything they understood, their grandparents, their school and their friends, to set up with a man they hardly knew in a totally different environment at the other end of the country. When Maureen was living at Washington in the early days of our relationship, the boys ran away, wanting to be with their dad, but in fairness they soon adapted to life on the South Coast and have always been a great credit to their mother, their father and their stepfather. I am as proud of them as if they were my own and all those tribulations were made worthwhile by the love of Maureen.

There were inevitable early problems, as much my fault as theirs. Neither of the boys is sporty and I could never comprehend why they always wanted to stay indoors when there was so much to do outside. I laugh about it now, but I used to lock them out of the house so they could get some fresh air. In addition, on Saturday mornings, match days, I needed peace and solitude to prepare myself for the game ahead but that seemed to be a cue for them to crash about the house, making as much noise as possible.

But these were minor grumbles from a period of re-adjustment for us all and we came through it. Our family was completed with the birth of Kate in 1983. The boys dote on her and so do we but she is all the more important to me because of the collapse of my relationship with Claire.

I could understand Julie being bitter. Her world had been smashed by my desertion and she too had to start again. But while she had custody of Claire, provision was made in the judge's ruling for me to visit my daughter whenever possible, bearing in mind that I was now living on the South Coast and for me to see Claire required a lot of travelling. On Saturdays after matches at The Dell, while my team-mates were enjoying a pint or two, either of my friends Bertie or John The Horse, as we knew them, would take me to Heathrow for an evening flight to the airport at Teesside. On Saturday evenings I would go out with Bobby Kerr and the plan was for me to meet Claire next day and take her out between 10am and 4pm, as the ruling had indicated I could. But by my estimation only about one in every ten times was I able to visit her without interruption or some barrier being put in the way.

Most occasions I never saw her at all. As Claire grew older her mother poisoned her against me and more often than not I would fly back to Heathrow not even having seen my daughter. I used to board that plane crying uncontrollably. Many a divorced father wonders what to do with their children when they have temporary custody and it's not easy to fill the time but I used to take Claire to mam's house until I realised all I was doing was babysitting for a few hours. Claire did meet Maureen and our kids and we always got on well, so there was never any tension, but Claire and I were never allowed to bond as daughter and father.

Julie eventually found an Irishman she wanted to marry and to be with him meant leaving the country so I took out an injunction to stop her doing that, later relenting when I knew my visiting rights were preserved. I always wanted Claire to come with my new family on holiday and it was agreed with Julie that I would fly to Belfast to pick up Claire at the airport there, take her back to England and then on to Minorca where we would be holidaying with Bertie and his wife, Sheila. But when I got to Belfast there was Julie with Claire and her new-born baby Lauren.

Julie was playing mind games. She could have sent Claire to the airport with her husband but when it came to the parting, Claire wanted to stay with her mother and refused to leave. There was nothing I could do in such a situation without making a scene but I knew Julie had set this up deliberately. I had the humiliation of turning round and boarding a plane for the trip back as tears ran down my cheeks. Later Claire changed her surname to that of her stepfather without telling me so that cards, presents and other mail never reached her. I still send her cards every Christmas and birthday to the last address I had for her but I never get any acknowledgement and I suppose we might never now have a relationship. I tried my best and I believe I did so with a clear conscience.

All I know of her is that Claire has a partner and two children, Lucas and Summer, my grandchildren. I have only met Lucas twice and Summer once. Maureen has been very supportive and did all she could to include her in our family. In addition her boys have always had a good rapport with their father and always saw him whenever they wanted, as should always be the case. Their dad, Howard Pearson, has been very much part of their lives, as have Howard's parents, Bob and Beatrice, and Maureen's parents, Paddy and Lilian. I wish Claire had been part of mine and I fear she missed out by not getting to know her stepbrothers and half-sister and being part of us. Even now I would say to Claire if I ever got the chance: there are two sides to every story. You are old enough to ask a few questions, be mature enough to listen. I would give you honest answers, a clear picture of what really happened without bitterness or rancour.

Justin is at the time of writing sales manager for the Carnival Group, one of the biggest cruising companies in the world, and lives in the Southampton area with his partner Joanne and our grandson, Harrison. Christian married in some style in India to Poornima, whom we know as Nicky, and they have a child, our granddaughter Asha. Kate is an accounts manager in Southampton and has a partner, Dylan. The extended family is a big one and probably because of what we went through at the start a close one. It is sad that Claire is not part of it, but there is still time and I hope for a reconciliation.

Maureen and I were married at Southampton register office on 16 September 1982. As I said, we had to move the date to accommodate one of my England involvements and Bobby Kerr, after what we had both been through, was a first-rate best man. It was a good way to close a stormy chapter in our lives and to begin the process of looking forward. Maureen has been a wonderful wife through thick and thin and has my love and admiration for the way she has coped with so much turmoil.

All through this I was trying to play football for Middlesbrough. There had been changes over the years as Jack's team evolved into John Neal's. In 1978/79, for instance, a year we finished 12th, Neal brought in a foreign player in Bosco Jankovic, a qualified lawyer from Yugoslavia. In recent years our team, while not exclusively from the North-East, didn't travel far for recruitment so a foreign player was probably someone from south of Nottingham.

In many ways Bosco took us into unknown territory. For a start he carried around a pouch, what would now be known as a man-bag, an object of some curiosity for his team-mates and not the sort of thing many men in Middlesbrough placed at the top of their Christmas list. Not unlike Dimitar Berbatov in many ways, strong but not especially quick, he was a real character and much loved by the Ayresome Park crowd. Bosco was a crowd-pleaser, a wonderful footballer and an inspired signing by Neal. The manager was trying to make us an attractive side to watch and I think the fans appreciated what he did. Micky Burns came in, so too Terry Cochrane, an exciting winger from Burnley for £233,333, and then Bosco in February for £100,000.

Some of the old guard were moving on, Cooper to Bristol City and Jim Platt loaned temporarily to Hartlepool and Cardiff, Maddren was forced by a knee injury to retire while Mills at last got away to West Bromwich in January 1979. I was sorry to see Mills go because we had been stalwarts together for many a year by this time. We played Newcastle at home once and of course the atmosphere was electric, as it was for all derby matches, and Mills was getting some stick from the Chicken Run, the popular part of our ground, for one or two errors. At one point a dog appeared from their midst and ran on to the pitch, eluding all attempts to catch it. The dog took a liking to Mills and started to follow him around. Every time Mills made a run, so too did the dog, like an additional marker. Eventually the dog was grabbed and taken away, at which point the fans chanted, 'Leave the dog on, take Mills off.'

Burns was a busy, intelligent player and he appreciated the way each of us played. Irishman Cochrane was what was known years ago as a 'tanner ball player', gifted but temperamental, lots of skill but always moaning if he didn't get the ball. He could and did beat the same defender three or four times, to the frustration of his team-mates so that he never quite fulfilled expectations.

Right at the start of the season, 26 August, we went down to Southampton and lost 2-1, a match in which I scored. The day was boiling hot and I wasn't used to the sun, or at least not to such intensity, and I didn't much like The Dell either. The fans seemed to be right on top of us, the pitch was hard and Saints were in our faces throughout so that it wasn't a particularly pleasant experience. We seemed to take ages to get down to Southampton and ages to get back. I remember thinking on the long journey back to Middlesbrough there was no way I would ever want to play for Southampton.

Once again I didn't miss a match, while breaking through about this time was Craig Johnston, who as I revealed, had been retained only on the intervention of George Wardle. Craig showed what could be achieved by sheer bloody-minded determination, returning in the afternoons to build up his slim physique and work on his technique. George kept him going through the dark days when he first arrived, told him to persevere and provided him with one valuable piece of advice: never show the opposition you're tired. Not the most gifted, Craig proved numerous fine judges wrong and I know he was forever grateful to George for seeing something in him others did not. Craig merely endorsed my own views of George, who as a teacher knew how to develop people through encouragement and cajoling and his masterly insight to the human condition made him a great psychologist.

I was top scorer in 1979/80 with 14, a decent figure for a midfield player, and I imagine it was one of the reasons why

England began to show an interest in me again. John Neal made sure we were always super fit, taking us off to Aberystwyth for some pre-season endurance work on the sands, staying at the university and it paid off with a handsome 3-1 win at Tottenham on the opening day. I always loved playing our first game of the season away because the expectation is heavily with the home side, especially with a club like Spurs who expected to challenge, and still expect to challenge, for honours. Fans build up their anticipation throughout the summer and then see them dashed on the first afternoon. I got one of the goals, Bosco got another and Burns the third and things got better when in the following game we beat Manchester City 3-0 as the prelude to one of our better seasons.

We were in the top ten most of the season, finishing ninth, and another highlight was drawing 1-1 at home to Manchester United. There were some 30,000 squeezed into Ayresome Park to see me get a second-half equaliser and only a great save from Gary Bailey denied me the winner. The one thing about playing United was that we never needed a team talk. Even during some lean years they were always the team to beat.

At one stage a place in the UEFA Cup beckoned after we got to fifth by the end of March, but we fell away thereafter by going seven matches without a win. Craggs and I were the only players to appear in every league game but we were starting to lose more of those who had become so important to the club over the good years. Boam had gone to Newcastle, Sunderland claimed Cummins for £100,000 and Mahoney had moved to Swansea. We were starting to become a selling club and the manager was becoming concerned. Who would be next?

I won't forget 1980/81 in a hurry. It was the season of my first cap in Sydney, the season my long run of consecutive appearances came to an end and it was the season I was awarded a testimonial at the age of 25. I was actually 26 when my testimonial match was played but it was very rare for a

Already winning football cups. David aged eleven scoops the major sporting prizes at Gilesgate New Junior School. The Middlesbrough scouts were already closing in.

Secretary Harry Green fails to suppress a devilish grin as I sign my first professional contract with Middlesbrough in 1972 aged 17. What made him smile was me agreeing to accept £20 a week.

We didn't get many photographers at Middlesbrough youth matches. But one managed to capture me as a 16-year-old lashing a goal past York City's goalkeeper.

Middlesbrough's full squad to include juniors and staff pictured in 1970. The young Armstrong, complete with hair, is in the front row on the right, not yet senior enough to earn a seat.

My mentor and lifestyle guide George Wardle at a Middlesbrough testimonial dinner. I owed so much to George and gave him one of my early England shirts to thank him.

Middlesbrough's first team squad in the John Neal era. Neal is on the far left and the 'Boro squad were in Jersey preparing for an FA Cup match.

David Armstrong aged 21 and looking pleased with life. So I should. I was established in the Middlesbrough team and was an England under 23 international.

The family gather at my testimonial at Middlesbrough. Left to right: My brother John, Dad Jack, Jack Charlton, and brothers Joseph and Billy.

Dad Jack, Mam Nora, and sisters Susan and Jeanette at my Middlesbrough testimonial reception. We were a close family then and we still are.

My close friend and later best man, Bobby Kerr should have been marking me as I score for Middlesbrough against Sunderland, my favourite team as I was growing up.

One against one takes on a whole new meaning here. I have somehow managed to evade my marker and every other player on the pitch while scoring this goal for Middlesbrough. Had they all gone home?

Middlesbrough v Arsenal at Highbury. John Hollins is on the ground and Liam Brady and team-mate Irving Nattrass can only admire my skill.

Studying the pre-match menu, or is it one of Jack Charlton's famous dossiers on our next opponents? Looking suitably unsure alongside myself are (from left) Peter Bickerstaff, Brian Taylor and Malcolm Smith.

Bobby Kerr and myself are pictured with James Bond. That really was his name. Note Bobby's Newcastle Brown Ale, shaken and not stirred.

Stuart Boam, the backbone of the Middlesbrough defence for years, shares my success in winning the North East player of the year award and wishes it was him.

The perfect penalty. The Sunderland goalkeeper is fooled by my smooth approach and goes the wrong way. Middlesbrough are a goal to the good and Roker Park, where I stood as a child, goes silent.

The three lions. Kevin Keegan, David Armstrong and Alan Ball in jovial mood.

England's squad of 1980. I'm in the second row on the left, pictured at a get-together at West Lodge, Cockfosters, London.

Lawrie McMenemy, later to sign me for Southampton, presents me with the first North East Football Writers' Association player of the year award in my home town. What could be better?

Bobby Robson leads an England training session. As usual with Bobby, I'm on the edge. Ray Wilkins, Alan Devonshire, Bryan Robson, Trevor Francis and Ricky Hill listen attentively, hoping he gets their names right. (BOB THOMAS PICTURE)

The England team which faced West Germany at Wembley in October, 1982. Back row (l to r): Shilton, Butcher, Thompson, Mabbutt, Regis, Devonshire. Front: Mariner, Wilkins, Armstrong, Sansom, Hill. (BOB THOMAS PICTURE)

England's squad go in search of divine help at the foot of Rio de Janeiro's famous Christ the Redeemer statue overlooking the city. It worked for John Barnes. (BOB THOMAS PICTURES)

Peter Shilton, later a Southampton colleague but then playing for Nottingham Forest, is beaten by my header. It hit the bar and I scored from the rebound.

When I retired from playing, I worked in Bournemouth's football-in-the-community office. Here I'm attending a seminar with Alan Curtis on the left and the former Blackpool and Coventry and Scottish international winger Tommy Hutchison in the centre.

This match was memorable because it was the first televised Match of the Day live on a Friday night. Southampton were playing Blackburn in the FA Cup. Here I'm scoring past sprawling ex-Saints goalkeeper Terry Gennoe. Glenn Keeley and Danny Wallace watch.

Ipswich were always a strong side in my time, credit to Bobby Robson. Left to right: Paul Cooper, Keegan, Stuart McCall, Mick Mills, Terry Butcher and Roger Osborne.

England v Denmark in Copenhagen, 22 September 1982. From the left in the England dug-out are Tony Woodcock, myself, Alvin Martin, Ricky Hill, Ray Clemence, Don Howe, Bobby Robson and Fred Street, our physio. I didn't get any action, again. (BOB THOMAS PIX)

Always proud to represent my country. This picture is dear to me because it was taken at what I consider to be the peak of my career.

Beating Manchester United was always special. This is my last-minute winner at the Dell. Paddy Roche is the goalkeeper and Gordon McQueen (6) is in the wrong place.

I say this was a diving headed goal against Arsenal. Or was it just a strong wind that day?

Rising to the occasion. Manchester United defenders Kevin Moran and Gordon McQueen (in the wrong place again) fail to stop me scoring with a header. Look how high I jumped.

Give me the ball. One of us is a Southampton all-time great. The other is Matt Le Tissier.

In my later role as charity dinner organiser. This one was the Wessex Cancer Trust's inaugural dinner. Some of the famous names (left to right) are Matt Le Tissier, Kevin Keegan, author Leslie Thomas and Tim Flowers. In the second row on the right is ex-referee Neil Midgeley.

With the family: David in the summer of 2013 with (clockwise from top left) Christian, Justin, Kate, David and Maureen.

player in his mid-20s to earn such an accolade and of course I was flattered.

Middlesbrough were often struggling for money at the time and Neal was becoming agitated by the way his best players were being sold from under him. Newcastle had taken Peter Johnson and Alan Ramage had gone to Derby and bigger clubs were circling round myself, Craig Johnston and one or two others. By awarding a testimonial, Middlesbrough were trying to stop me joining the growing exodus. To be honest I was not bothered about the money, my first wife got all of that anyway, I just wanted an acknowledgement from the club of my worth to them. I wanted to be appreciated.

I was growing uneasy at the way the likes of Souness and Mills had been allowed to go and not been replaced and getting first into the England B side and then the full international team made me realise that there was a life outside Middlesbrough and that it wouldn't take much to find another, more glamorous club. I had after all been at Middlesbrough since I was nine and in the first team since I was 17 so in terms of experience and matches played I was due some reward. Normally it's lads of 35 or 36, coming to the end of their careers and facing uncertain futures who are awarded a testimonial season, which in addition to a match includes dinners and other fund-raising activities. It means a busy year with lots of social activity but mine was coinciding with the chaos of my home life and the subsequent breakdown of my marriage. So it was never straightforward and once or twice a little awkward.

My testimonial match was played in front of a crowd of 10,000, who as always showed their great support for me, and it was preceded by a match involving my pals from Durham. A team of celebrities played against New Durham Club and Durham Boilers, whom I had coached and for whom playing in front of such a big crowd was a chance to shine. But, as I say, the money soon disappeared.

This was a great year for me on the field. I was eventually fans' player of the year to go with my first England cap and I felt that I was absolutely on top of my game. I doubt that I ever played better in my life or consistently so well. I was still young and yet battle-hardened and increasingly canny and I think perhaps only Bosco outshone me, finishing with 13 goals and regularly catching the eye, never more so than at home to Ipswich on the penultimate day of the season. Bobby Robson's Ipswich were a hair's breadth from the league title but we beat them 2-1 and Bosco got both goals, leaving their championship hopes in tatters.

In September 1980 a rare event took place, namely a Middlesbrough football match without David Armstrong taking part in it. After playing in the first four I was injured and missed the next two against Nottingham Forest and Sunderland. I am 'ashamed' to admit that I missed a third in March, ironically against Southampton, because of that Geoff Palmer tackle in the FA Cup. I could have missed more but played through the worst of the injury.

My first absence meant that my run of 305 league matches, 365 in all competitions, dating back to March 1973 had come to a halt, some seven years and five months since a Middlesbrough team had last gone on to the pitch without me. Of course I'm proud of my achievement but much had changed over those seven years and five months. Only the seemingly indestructible Craggs and the reinstated Platt remained from when I started.

But while my career was taking off a little, the club were going through difficult times. We finished 14th and in May 1981 Neal resigned when Craig Johnston was sold to Liverpool for £575,000. Middlesbrough needed the money and Neal couldn't face losing another major player. Bobby Murdoch was promoted from youth coach and while I had great respect for Bobby as a supreme player, he struggled to continue Neal's fine work. I was sorry to see Neal go, not least because the discipline which he had imposed was breaking down rapidly under the new regime. Apprentices no longer held their seniors in proper regard and all the good habits drilled into me at an early age no longer seemed to apply. Things were changing and not for the better.

I think when Johnston was sold I realised I too had to go but it was not going to be straightforward breaking the umbilical cord. I suppose the exposure to players from other clubs had opened my eyes a little and I realised that if I was to have an international career it might be better served by a club more often in the hunt for honours. My off-field problems were coming to a head and I came to the sad and inevitable conclusion that I had to move on.

And the red Mercedes? It was while I was test-driving it that Maureen and I spotted the house we still live in at Fair Oak. But the car was soon sold during hard financial times which followed my transfer. My little plan to make sure money from my testimonial didn't get to my first wife failed to work out.

9

Rejecting Manchester United

MANCHESTER UNITED were keen to sign me once I had decided to leave Middlesbrough but I chose Southampton instead. Today that would be regarded as a very strange decision, especially at the way United have gone on to become a major world super-power, winning all there was to be won under Sir Alex Ferguson while Southampton dipped for a year or two into League 1 after becoming embroiled in unsustainable money problems.

Ron Atkinson was manager of Manchester United at the time, the summer of 1981, and I never got as far as speaking to him or anyone at United but there was genuine interest. What I didn't realise was that Middlesbrough were fast running out of money and the constant sales of key players, which had driven John Neal to resign, was only being used to satisfy debts. It was my turn to follow a string of top class players out of Ayresome Park. I am not sure why Middlesbrough were struggling to cope but once it became clear I wanted to go they didn't make much of an effort to get me to change my mind. They needed the money I would fetch in the transfer market.

I understand Atkinson offered cash plus Mike Duxbury, a young defender who had made his debut the year before but was not yet established. Middlesbrough turned it down without giving it much thought. They wanted cash alone and weren't bothered about any player makeweight. It is a shame for them because Duxbury later became an important member of the United team which won the FA Cup twice and went on to earn ten England caps. Had Middlesbrough accepted Atkinson's offer they would have received money and a player they might have developed and sold on at a later date. But life is full of chances missed and taken and it simply never happened.

I should emphasise that in 1981 United were still coming back from some lean years in the 1970s, trying to recapture the golden era of Best, Law and Charlton. It is true United had been league runners-up a year or two before and Atkinson had brought in Bryan Robson and Mark Hughes but it was not until Ferguson came along that the club was restored to greatness. In contrast Lawrie McMenemy's Southampton was a club on the way up. They had Keegan, twice European Player of the Year when at Hamburg, Channon, Ball and a collection of high class players supporting them and everyone wanted to play for them. I had no hesitation once the move was put in place and I have to say 30 or so years later that I have had no regrets about my decision. Southampton was right for me then and is still right for me now.

For a start, the weather is better but there was far more to it than that. I liked the club, the fans, other players, the manager, the countryside and even the rickety old Dell. Having said that about the south which is now home, I still love going back to the North-East. At Scotch Corner the hairs on the back of my neck (yes, I still have a few) rise and there is no finer sight in my mind than Durham Castle and Cathedral approached from the

A690. I still have many friends on Teesside and in Durham and Maureen and I are always given a wonderful welcome when we return, as we often do.

Our move to the South Coast was influenced obviously by what had been going on in our private lives so that moving to Southampton gave us a fresh start and the possibility of a new life.

As the start of the 1981/82 season approached I reported to Middlesbrough for pre-season training not knowing how much longer I would be there. Murdoch was running his first pre-season and had brought in Joe Bolton from Sunderland as his major signing but it was quickly clear to me that the intensity and focus had gone. I thought back to George Wardle, to Stan Anderson, to Jack Charlton, to his hard-man assistant Ian McFarlane, a loud Scottish coach who made us jump at his every command, and I could see that everything they stood for in terms of discipline, selfless hard work and ambition to succeed had drained away almost overnight. It broke my heart to see what was happening but it strengthened my resolve to get away.

Middlesbrough were no longer the club I had joined and I knew that if I stayed there any longer I would achieve nothing, my level of performance would drop and I would eventually become unhappy. So I asked the club to be put on the transfer list with great reluctance. They had brought me through, given me my chance to play in the First Division and rewarded me with a testimonial. On the other hand I had done everything for them on and off the pitch as an ambassador and gone almost eight years without missing a game. I felt I owed them nothing and they certainly didn't owe me anything, except the chance to get away.

It wasn't generally known that I wanted to go, there was nothing about it in the local or national press at first, and I heard only through the grapevine once my name had been circulated to other clubs that Leeds, managed by Allan

Clarke, were interested while Tottenham were also keen. At 26, with more than 400 matches behind me and now a full-blown international, I was a good catch for someone and I was determined to make sure the next move would be the right one. I was at a crossroads in more ways than one.

Harold Shepherdson always kept a paternal eye on me and it was he who first alerted me to Southampton's interest, 'Lawrie McMenemy wants to talk to you, would you like to meet him?' I can't pretend it wasn't a shock. Leeds, Tottenham, Manchester United, I had half expected them, but Southampton were not a club I had considered. The clubs had apparently agreed a fee of £600,000, a record for them both, so it was a question of whether or not I would be keen in going that far south. I thought back to that long, hot trip to The Dell, the hostility of the crowd and the quality of their players and my first question was, 'How do I get there?'

Then it all happened so quickly, almost in a blur. I got a lift to Durham station where an old friend of mine, Alan 'Tat' Whitfield, was in the ticket office. 'I'm going to London. Give me the best seat for the cheapest price,' I said to him. I barely had time to tell Maureen and before I knew it I was on my way to the Royal Garden Hotel in Kensington where I was to meet McMenemy and Saints' financial director, Guy Askham.

As the North-Eastern countryside slipped behind me and we approached London, I wondered what I had let myself in for. I barely had time to gather my wits before Lawrie was putting an arm round my shoulder and sweet-talking me. Lawrie enjoyed a big profile at the time as one of the bright young managers, articulate, personable and much-loved by television where he was a shrewd and descriptive analyst, his booming Geordie voice making him one of the most recognisable figures in English football.

I have a lot of time for Lawrie and in 1981 he was building the best side Southampton ever had. I was flattered that he even thought I might be able to improve it, but it seemed an ideal move in so many ways. All I most wanted to do was put my family problems behind me and play football for a good team. And Southampton were a very good team. Lawrie said all the right things about living in a nice area, playing with so many great players and how they and the fans, the club's unofficial 12th man, seemed to enjoy their football. Saints were about to embark on a European campaign, something of course I had never experienced or was likely to at Middlesbrough, and it all just seemed like a wonderful opportunity.

My only regret was that I sold myself short. As Lawrie told me how I was the right man for him, how I would give the team balance and other flattering things, I should have played harder to get. Desperate just to get started, I agreed to the salary offer of £35,000 a year. Within weeks, stripped of every asset by a judge, I realised I should have asked for a great deal more than I was getting. I shouldn't have been so keen.

Anxious to make sure there were no last-minute hitches and to prevent any rival clubs coming in with counter-offers, I was put on a train almost immediately from Waterloo to Winchester, about an hour away, where I was met by Southampton's secretary, Brian Truscott, and driven on to The Dell, reaching the deserted ground at 10pm on a Friday. Chris Lawrence, the club's doctor, was there to carry out a medical, which I passed, and Truscott scuttled off to get the transfer forms. At the end of a long and unexpected day I was a Southampton player and settled in for the rest of the night at the Southampton Park Hotel, trying to come to terms with what I had done. Only then, when all had been completed, did Lawrie announce to the world another transfer coup.

I don't rank mine with that of Kevin Keegan, whom Lawrie had lured in secret from Germany to a hotel near Romsey and then produced him from behind a curtain with the panache of a conjuror and to the shock of the assembled press, but he had this remarkable habit of persuading an endless list of quality footballers to play for him over a ten-year period when the club challenged for every honour. He sold them the vision of the club's future as he had done to me and I can't think of anyone before or since who has been so masterful and so successful in the transfer market on such a scale.

I understand from figures not so long ago released that a top flight player at around the time I was playing for Southampton would be earning between £400 and £500 a week. At least I was earning more than that but those same figures reveal that the average wage in the Premier League in 2010 was more than £22,000 a week. I was definitely born 20 years too soon in that respect.

I headed back to the North-East later that weekend to begin the process of moving and saying goodbye to my Middlesbrough 'family'. A family they had been. From the age of nine when George Wardle first spotted my potential I had never wanted to play for anyone else. I could have gone to Revie's Leeds or Burnley, as I revealed, as a talented child but stuck with Middlesbrough, learned personal and professional discipline I might never have learned elsewhere, and enjoyed 17 fantastic years with the club.

We were a whisker away from being an outstanding team in Jack Charlton's second year but all that seemed a long way off when I went back in on the Monday, three days after joining Southampton to collect my boots and shake a few hands. To a man they wished me well, not one of my ex-colleagues thought I had made a mistake. It was a sad day, turning my back on everything I had known and cared about, but it had to be done. I am not sure if there were tears in my eyes as I slipped away but it felt like a parting. If I had been an itinerant, shifting from club to club on a regular basis, it might not have hurt as much as it did but it was hard leaving Middlesbrough, I can't deny. I had this awful feeling they would struggle, not that I would necessarily have made much difference, and they did, finishing last and winning only eight of their 42 league matches. I drew no satisfaction in that. The problem was that Middlesbrough had become a selling club and no one can keep selling their best players and expect to survive.

Anyway, I was required to start training at Southampton and drove back down in my Tom Cowie-sponsored car, a vehicle I was later obliged to hand back and replace with the notorious red Mercedes.

I was just pleased that Maureen was happy to go along with this quite revolutionary plan to uproot and move to a different part of the country with the boys in tow. There is no doubt, having lived equally in both areas, the North-East and on the South Coast, that they are in so many ways very different, not better or worse, just different and it's not always easy to adjust. I at least had my new team-mates but when Maureen came down she knew no one and it says a lot for her strength of character that she soon came to terms with her new environment and thrived.

It was good that we were to be together as a couple, as a family, but it wasn't an easy start, a seven-hour drive before settling into rented accommodation, found for us by Lawrie in Glen Eyre Road in Southampton for the next three months. Maureen never complained and would have been happy to have gone anywhere. Her only stipulation was that the boys should see their father regularly. I was more than happy with that arrangement. Later on, we found our present home and we have always been happy in it. The cricketers Chris and Robin Smith lived nearby and were briefly social friends. So far, so good.

But it didn't last long. The problem was that my past was catching up with me. I may now have been in deepest Hampshire but the divorce settlement made on Teesside had a brutal effect. To the outside world it may have looked as if

Maureen and I had everything we wanted; a nice house, a good salary, each other. But how many other England footballers had bailiffs knocking at the door as I did? You read about top players who got into difficulties with drink, drugs, fast women and slow horses but in my case I couldn't afford to buy a pint of milk for no other reason than that I had been the financial victim of a messy divorce. If I had been a boozer, a serial womaniser or handed over a fortune to the bookies I would have held my hand up and admitted the error of my ways. All I had done was marry the wrong woman at the wrong time. Yes, I was earning £35,000 a year but that was before tax and then I had to pay Julie £15,000 of what remained.

We got to the stage where we had to be careful what we spent on food and at the time I was very grateful to Ian Butcher who worked for the Dorset brewers, Hall and Woodhouse. Ian took pity on us and generously donated soft drinks so that I could pay my milk bill to Les, our milkman. It was embarrassing, humiliating, incredible that I, an England player, a First Division footballer, a hero to some, should need to barter with a tradesman just to make sure I could feed my new family the essentials of daily living.

One day as this torment bit into us, there was a knock on the door of our new home. It was the bailiffs. They wanted to take away our furniture in lieu of money owed because I had apparently defaulted in the payment for Julie's legal costs. I had to prevent them physically making off with what little we owned between us. After all, Julie had kept the contents of our marital home and Maureen too had been forced to abandon most of her furniture in the North-East. Only after a lot of pleading was I able to convince them that I could meet my debt.

I was asked to report to the bailiffs' offices in Winchester and make the payment required. We were only able to do that because Maureen had received a settlement from her husband which allowed us to escape another visit from the 'heavies'.

It was as well for us that Howard, Maureen's husband, was not as vindictive as Julie had been but life was no easier when it came to Christmas, the traditional time for goodwill and present-giving. We were so poor that we couldn't afford to give each other presents and the boys had to make do with socks and other such 'useful' items. At least we had some good friends who by now could see our difficulties and came to our aid, mindful that just because of my professional status I was not rolling in money. Our special thanks here to Caroline and Dieter Dent, a couple we had met in Winchester soon after our arrival, Ian and Linda Butcher, who helped us financially and emotionally in difficult times and also Stan and Jean Davies, Dawn and Graham Bailey and Bill and Jean Laidlaw.

Poor Maureen, transplanted to a part of the country she knew nothing about and with a new family to support, went out to work and three decades later is still working as hard as ever. We will both be grafting until we are 90 at this rate because money remains tight.

I have to admit we didn't help ourselves. There was an opportunity to open a fashion shop in Basingstoke with John The Horse and we decided it was a risk worth taking because Maureen knew about fashion and it would provide her with a job. So we re-mortgaged our home and sunk some money into the venture only for it to collapse within a year. Maureen later worked at another fashion shop, Foxy Lady in Shamrock Quay, not far from Southampton's present ground at St Mary's. She now sells office supplies to American government bases, a role which takes her all over the country.

All through this, Southampton were aware of our financial problems and while they didn't at that stage offer to increase my wages, they were at least sympathetic. Lawrie gave me vouchers for the children and Maureen to go on holiday at a Pontins resort in Spain because there was no other way they could have gone. My own holidays consisted of wherever Saints were on tour, pre-season or post-season so while my team-mates at Southampton enjoyed a good standard of living, typical of young men being paid well to do something they enjoyed, we were watching what we ate. The only good to come out of this occasionally dire situation is that we came across friends who have remained so.

There is always a danger that when you are a footballer, a recognisable personality, you draw people to you who only want a bit of reflected glory and disappear when your star fades. But happily we fell among people who liked us for ourselves, many of whom, like Maureen, knew nothing about football and cared less. After a hard game, it was always pleasant to be with people who didn't want to talk about football.

By now in my mid-20s I was one of the most recognisable footballers in the country, and I say that without conceit. My playing era coincided with big hair and I had none at all, at least next-to-none, from an early age. It has never been a problem. Dad was bald at an early age and my own hair was fine so I came to the conclusion quite early in life that I would go the same way. Nowadays I wouldn't stand out in the way I did when I was playing because there are any number of 'skinheads' either through genuine baldness or as a fashion statement. In fact I loved it when the opposition or the opposition's fans started to deride me as a 'bald bastard'. I used to pretend to run my hands through where my hair should have been and laughed and in its way my appearance made me stand out and be more noticeable.

But there has been a downside to my premature loss of hair. Not so long ago I was diagnosed with skin cancer. My long exposure to the elements had led to scabs and marks on my head turning cancerous, but luckily I'm able to play this down because it's not life-threatening now that I rub a special cream into the scalp.

My baldness also had an upside because I was easy to spot. In 1986 we got a great deal through Justin in which we went to New York by QE2, stayed at the world-famous Waldorf Hotel with our friends Adrian and Lyn English and flew back by Concorde in three hours and 18 minutes. Once ensconced in the hotel, we ventured outside and I hailed a taxi, whereupon to my great surprise, the taxidriver looked me over and said, 'Are you David Armstrong?' I thought I had been set-up and started laughing, looking around for a culprit. But it turned out the driver was a Greek-American who watched *Match of the Day* and recognised me from that. Fancy that, a boy from Sherburn Road, picked out in the centre of New York.

He took us off to Greenwich Village all the happier for having met a global footballing superstar. I don't think so, but I do have football to thank for taking me around the world three or four times. I have been to Australia three times for instance and some other countries I have visited only fleetingly because you tended as a player to arrive at a destination, train, play and go again in a day or two without having the chance to explore.

In October 1981, three months after my move to Southampton and with my world upended by my crippling divorce, my beloved dad died at the age of 69. My parents had not been party to my sudden and swift departure from Middlesbrough so you can imagine their reaction when I rang to tell them where I was now. Just before dad died I had arranged for them to make the journey south to see us and to get a taste of our new life. They were looking forward to it but first they went on holiday to Blackpool and it was there that he collapsed and died in a bed and breakfast. There had been no indication of anything untoward with his heart so it was another devastating setback at a time when I needed all the support I could get.

I carried on playing, but I'm not sure how. I was in a daze for weeks on end, going through the motions, trying to piece together the bits of a life in turmoil. The whole extended family were shocked because dad had been fit and had been looking forward to coming to Southampton to see his son playing alongside the great Kevin Keegan and all our other big names, but sadly he never got the chance.

As I said, I still possess those first football boots he bought for me, which must have been a sacrifice because he was never well off. My parents were always available to me, always on my side and to lose my father at such a juncture in my life was another massive blow.

Moving from Middlesbrough to Southampton in playing terms was a colossal cultural change. I went from being a proud member of a compact, slowly changing little unit to a bit-part player in football's equivalent of the Harlem Globetrotters. While my first match was a friendly at Plymouth, the first chance I got to know the rest of the Saints squad was on a pre-season tour of Spain where as part of my initiation I was obliged to sing a song in front of the rest of the squad. As a devoted follower of Creedence Clearwater Revival, a big band at the time, I might have chosen something from their repertoire but in the end I plumped for 'A Thousand Conversations' by Hank Marvin, Bruce Welch and John Farrar and, clearing my throat, I got through it. Not being outgoing this was a bit of an ordeal but that moment in Seville was the start of a fascinating six-year experience.

Everything about Southampton at the time was extrovert. The manager, a ramrod-straight ex-guardsman, enjoyed a nationwide reputation for his television appearances which included adverts for non-alcoholic beers and was as much a larger-than-life individual as his players. He encouraged their individuality and the players acknowledged the freedom he gave them by producing any number of truly wonderful performances. It was a joy to be among them. Of course it was a shock to my system because at Middlesbrough our strength often lay in the team ethic, subjugating our personal preferences and pride for the sake of the collective achievement.

At Southampton it was the opposite. We were encouraged to be different, to express ourselves as players and to enjoy what we did. Lawrie was clever like that. He could have been intimidated by the big names but he let them have their head. And there were some big, big egos. Add Ivan Golac, the marauding right-back from Yugoslavia who didn't do anything he didn't want to do, and Steve Williams, a strong-willed midfield player, to Channon, Ball and Keegan and you had a potentially volatile mix. They could all be a handful, all thought they were number one, but when it came to a match they were all ultra-professional, all responsible and fiercely determined to preserve their reputations. It all took a bit of getting used to, the sheer cavalier approach after years of controlled rigidity.

After every home game, for instance, the big names would gather in the bar after matches, which in those days we had usually won, and belt out a rendition of 'New York, New York', pints in hand, as entertaining off the pitch as they had been on it. Larry the taxi driver was our DJ and the singing went on into the evening. So brilliant was their football, Lawrie never minded and neither did anyone else. Then I discovered training was a moveable feast. It all depended if there was a racehorse meeting somewhere within striking distance of Southampton. Channon, of course, went on to become an outstanding trainer and loved his racing probably more than his football, he has often admitted, while Keegan and Bally were enthusiastic punters who were just as keen to get on the road once our training was over for the day.

The essence of our training at whatever time of day was very concentrated, functional work always aimed at getting our world-class players into attacking positions. The message was to get forward at every opportunity and to hurt the opposition where it mattered. We probably conceded more goals than we should have done but that was because we all loved to be pressing towards the opposition goal. Other clubs laboured for three hours a day, maybe more, but such was the intensity of our own sessions that none of us could have lasted three hours. It was the quality we aimed for, not the quantity.

All those big names were fantastic workers in training but at noon or soon after they were gone. There were early-season days when Lawrie's military background insisted we gained basic fitness with eight-mile runs but while the fit and enthusiastic Nick Holmes often finished first, it was noticeable how Keegan and Ball were right up there with him.

We all looked forward to our Friday morning five-a-side matches in the Dell gymnasium. They were special and will be remembered by all those who took part in them forever, and not always with affection by those of us forced to wear the dreaded yellow jersey. In the Tour de France, the yellow jersey is much coveted but in our games it signified the worst player voted by the others during that session and no one wanted to be chosen. To put it bluntly this was the one day of the week when we kicked seven bells out of each other with an incredible intensity, bordering on the hostile. There were fights, players slammed into walls, noses pressed into boards, furious outbursts, everything that on the eve of a match should have completely destroyed morale and team spirit.

Lawrie's assistant, Lew Chatterley, was a lenient referee, but oddly no one got injured and in among all the sweat and the fury it actually brought us together as a unit. Even the quiet lads got stuck in, a chance for them to get their own back once in a while, and grudges were satisfied. It brought the worst out of us on a Friday but on Saturday it helped to bring out the best. I reckon it sparked us, made us alert, got rid of aggression and aided the gelling process.

All of this took me by surprise after Middlesbrough's more conventional approach to life but there was one lasting memory of their clash of egos. Channon, Keegan and Ball were exceptional players but they each liked to think they were number one. They had each been significant England internationals, Bally winning a World Cup, as he frequently told us, Keegan and Channon each finishing with 21 England goals. At any other club one of them would have been top dog but at Southampton this obviously wasn't possible. They did, however, find ways of outdoing each other.

They each wanted to be last on the team coach, homeward-bound from away matches. If one got on and found he was not last he would get off again and wait. This rampant display of one-upmanship annoyed the rest of us sitting patiently in our seats because our departure was often unnecessarily delayed until such time as they were all in place. It was always fascinating to see which of them 'won' but, that aside, they all got along famously, were great technical footballers with tremendous flair and it was a privilege to be their team-mate.

10

Lawrie's Unrewarded Vision

LAWRIE MCMENEMY has been badly treated by Southampton. There is a fine statue commemorating Ted Bates outside St Mary's and very deserving it is too. Ted took the club from the Third Division to the First Division and nurtured such club legends as Terry Paine, Ron Davies and Martin Chivers. But the man who made Southampton a big club was Lawrie and yet you would never know he existed if you visited the plush, modern 32,000-seat stadium. To be honest I think this is a travesty and the club should be ashamed of themselves for ignoring his incredible achievements.

Under Lawrie, Saints, previously a provincial club with no great pretensions, won the FA Cup, were runners-up in the League Cup, came second in the First Division and regularly played in European competition. But there was far more to his influence than bare statistics. The Southampton of today, the stadium, the big transfer fees, one of the best youth academies in the country, the high profile, was all put in place by the clarity of vision and the ambition of Lawrie McMenemy.

I know he made a few enemies when he left the club the first time for Sunderland and walking out on the same day as Graeme Souness didn't help ingratiate him with supporters on a second occasion, but now is the time to forget those blemishes and not let them mar what he did for the club.

At the time of writing John Mortimore is the club president and while I agree John had an outstanding career which included a spell as manager of Benfica, he never did for Saints what Lawrie did. Ask Saints fans of a certain age and they will say the football produced in the Kevin Keegan era, both immediately before and after as well, was the finest the club has ever produced. It was a privilege and a joy for me to be part of it and other players of that time will say the same. Why it is then that Lawrie, now in retirement a few miles from the city, is so down-played by the club he inherited from Bates and transformed briefly into England's most glamorous club?

Keegan, for one, would never have joined Saints had McMenemy not been there. I know Alan Ball felt the same way. Then comes a long list of top players who, like me, were queuing up to join Saints. Remember, we were not playing at Old Trafford, Anfield or Highbury but the shambling Dell which was not even a very good advert for the Third Division. Yet Peter Shilton, Dave Watson, Chris Nicholl, Mick Mills and many other high class internationals didn't need a moment's persuasion to come to play in it and call it home. The reason they did was Lawrie McMenemy.

It wasn't as though he was offering us massive wages with which our rivals could not compete. He wasn't offering us the trappings of a major footballing force. He offered them what he offered me, the concept of a club on the rise, the chance to play an uninhibited, free-rolling, cavalier brand of football unfettered by expectation or weighed down by history. There wasn't a player among us who didn't love playing for Southampton and I do mean love. Lawrie was always fair and open in his dealings with players when he was trying to sign them. There was no deceit, no hidden agenda, no promises which could not be fulfilled.

It can't have been easy managing and soothing some large egos but he knew what he was doing, trusting players to act in a mature and professional manner. Lawrie didn't mind his star names rushing off to race meetings after training as long as they had given everything beforehand and, as I explained, they certainly did that. Lawrie didn't have a playing background above non-league level but he had served his apprenticeship at Doncaster (where he was sacked) and Grimsby and he brought to his management style a maturity, a depth of knowledge about people and an ability to get the best out of each of us, bearing in mind our incredible individual diversity. Mortimore, Chatterley, Ian Branfoot and Dave Merrington carried out his orders as his faithful lieutenants but Lawrie organised the sessions and the tactics, carried out the signings and ran the club from top to bottom. Yet he was criticised even then for signing so many attacking players. Chris Nicholl, ever the natural defender, could be heard in matches urging us to come back and defend but his warnings fell on deaf ears more often than not.

The buzz surrounding the club at that time was electrifying, a constant sort of party atmosphere, much of it generated by Keegan who had this incredible aura about him and there wasn't a player among us who didn't look forward to the next game. Keegan had this capacity to inspire the rest of the team by sheer example in training and on the pitch and Lawrie was shrewd enough to let him have his head until one final, unfortunate incident. It was in his second season, my first, when the exasperated manager told Keegan he was cheating the fans during a half-time blasting, if memory serves, accusing him in effect of lack of effort during our home defeat by Aston Villa.

The one thing the competitive Kevin was not was a cheat. Even in friendlies he always gave 100 per cent; that was how he became Europe's best player. It was an ill-chosen word and we all heard it and I'm sure Lawrie must now regret it with hindsight, but the damage had been done. Kevin didn't travel with us to our next match at Swansea, making his own way, still smarting from the accusation. I think that can now be seen as the point of breakdown in their professional relationship and the beginning of the end of his commitment to Southampton. At the conclusion of that season late in the summer of 1982 Kevin left for Newcastle and it was a big shock for those he left behind and a setback for the club.

Without Lawrie, Southampton would not be where they are today. Look at the players the club have produced from their youth scheme. In recent years there has been Gareth Bale, Theo Walcott, Alex Oxlade-Chamberlain, Wayne Bridge and many others but their success is the legacy of the scheme put in place when Lawrie was at the helm. Until he came along Southampton recruited from their immediate environment but Lawrie put a scouting system in place that enabled us to bring the likes of Alan Shearer all the way down from Newcastle as a 16-year-old, Rod and Danny Wallace from London and a certain Matt Le Tissier from Guernsey.

There were many others, a high percentage of them either becoming Saints stalwarts or who were sold at a profit to other clubs at a lower level. Not only were we competing on the pitch against the big clubs, under Lawrie we were competing for the best young players in the country. These lads came down to the South Coast because Southampton was seen to be a great club to be playing for, a place where they would be encouraged to be themselves and where opportunities were guaranteed for the best of them. Not bad for a hitherto little club in the sticks.

One of Lawrie's shrewdest appointments was that of Jack Hixon to scout the North-East for us. Shearer was one of several wonderful prospects he pointed in our direction. Neil Maddison came at the same time as Shearer but there were others like Tony Sealy, George Shipley, Steve Davis and Tommy Widdrington who thought nothing of deserting their homes in the north to play for Lawrie's club. Other lads who came down as youngsters included Alan Knill, Chris Wilder and Phil Parkinson who went on to become respected coaches and managers.

Everyone wanted to play for us, everyone in the game was talking about us and for a few heady years under his stewardship we were the most attractive club in the league. That legacy remains. Even in the dark days of Rupert Lowe and the financial problems, the youth scheme was still churning out quality young footballers and still is. This is Lawrie's doing and has never been properly recognised. I am not denigrating Bates, Mortimore or sundry other people who have contributed to the Southampton of today. Even Rupert Lowe oversaw the stadium development. But Lawrie stands head and shoulders above them all for what he did for the club and I am not alone among ex-players who find it mystifying and not a little hurtful that his part in it all has been airbrushed from the club's history.

My first year with Saints was typical. We finished outside the top positions in the league and went out of the cups at an early stage but the adventures we had along the way will never be forgotten. Kevin got 28 goals that season, 1981/82, I got 15 from midfield and later that season we signed a lanky, raw, red-headed young defender called Mark Wright from Oxford. He was one for the future.

Having come from Middlesbrough where I was just about king of the midfield, I expected to take all the free kicks as I had done there. But when I got to Southampton I was at the bottom of a very long queue, behind Ball, Keegan and Channon inevitably and Steve Williams once in a while. All the big names wanted to have a go at dead ball situations. I got a bit fed up being shoved aside every time we got a free kick in sight of the opposition goal but as the new boy I had to bide my time.

Determined not to be bullied, we were awarded a free kick in a dangerous position against Swansea and, spotting a gap, I drilled the ball into the net, not waiting for a 'my ball' call from one of the others. It was a small triumph, showing all the big personalities I was not there to make up the numbers.

One of the highlights of that season was a 3-2 win over Manchester United at The Dell early in December. I got the winner in the last minute, running from our 18-yard box in support of Channon, timing my run perfectly, making the most of a defender's deflection and passing the ball into the net. But for me and countless others the match will be remembered for what Keegan described as the 'best goal I never scored'.

Unfortunately I played a prominent role in the incident. We all gasped at Wayne Rooney's sensational overhead kick against Manchester City in 2011, but Keegan did exactly the same in this match, a wonderful effort, the goal of the 20th century (or so he still says), the ball hooked over his shoulder into the United net with the goalkeeper motionless. The crowd took off, Keegan raced away to celebrate and then we all noticed the linesman flagging for offside. What fool had strayed offside? Me, as it turned out. In these days the goal would have stood because I was not interfering with play and even then it should have been allowed in the spirit of the game. There was no way my presence on the periphery of the action influenced the defensive actions but rules are rules and the change to them in this particular situation has been a big improvement. Kevin has never forgiven me and I think I only partially redeemed myself by scoring the late winner.

In January 1982 I made a sentimental return to Middlesbrough for the first time since my transfer and it was an unnerving experience, seeing all the players and staff I had left behind, knowing that we were flying at the top of the league and relegation was already a real prospect for them. Before the match Lawrie asked me if I wanted to be captain for the day against my old club but I was happy to let Kevin keep it since we were doing so well anyway. I need not have worried about what reception I might get from Middlesbrough fans because they applauded me as warmly as they ever did, maybe a little less enthusiastically after we had won 1-0 to go top of the First Division for the first time in our 97-year history.

After the game, the big three, all of course major punters, got us together to persuade us to put all the players' pool money, cash derived from outside sources, on us to win the First Division as a bet, although I forget the odds. In our euphoria at going top and now into the second half of the season, we decided as a team to go along with it. We finished seventh. We might have stood a chance of breaking a bookie's heart had the prolific Moran stayed fit but a back injury ruled him out from January onwards and we badly missed his goals. He was out for nine months.

Not that we could complain about goals because we got plenty of them including five against Coventry at The Dell in May and we were still not on the winning side. The match ended 5-5, the first anywhere in the league to end that way since 1966. Keegan scored twice for us and Mark Hateley, one day to play for AC Milan and England, got two for Coventry including the last-minute equaliser. We got into the dressing room shell-shocked, so shell-shocked that Danny Wallace was convinced we had lost 5-4. He needed to be told we had got a draw, albeit a crazy one.

Wright got three games towards the end of the season as the prelude to a long and successful career and we could see from the start that he was an exceptional player, awkward and leggy at times, but quick, strong, good in the tackle and blessed with pace. He was a good 'spot' by Lawrie's scouts in Oxford's reserves. There was another side to him, a cockiness as a youth which tended occasionally to arrogance later, but there was no denying that here was a real prospect.

Wright, Channon, George Lawrence and myself later had the strange experience of playing on loan for CB Hong Kong in a bid, fruitless as it turned out, to save them from relegation and there was no doubt that playing for Southampton opened all kinds of unlikely doors.

That summer Channon and Keegan departed and I don't think we were ever quite the same force or the same club, although we certainly had our moments later. How do you replace players of that calibre? Channon had spent, to that point, his entire career with the club but Lawrie felt he was getting on a bit and got him a move to Manchester City, mindful that in the wings he had the young Danny Wallace coming through strongly. As it turned out Mick was far from finished, did well at Maine Road and returned to Southampton later for a second stint. It was a calculated risk by the manager and there will be those who will say we should have kept him. To lose Keegan at the same time was a double blow and our supporters had to come to terms with the fact that we had lost simultaneously two of the greatest England players ever produced.

While Mick Channon's love for horses would keep him in the players' lounge watching the racing right up to kick-off time, he was revered for what he did on the pitch once he had got over the white line. Kevin remains one of my favourite players and one of my favourite people, a truly genuine man who had time for everyone. There was no queue of autograph-hunters too long, even after he had been pick-pocketed in southern Ireland while diligently working his way through one such line, and it was always a pleasure to be around his dynamism. He gave us a one-man feel-good factor and a national profile which was never replicated.

Keegan was just about the only Saints player with any experience of Europe and our lack of knowledge counted against us when we took part in the UEFA Cup. Our blistering attacking style was completely wrong for Europe where it was essential to be a lot more cagey. The first round was simple enough, a 3-0 win in Limerick followed by a 1-1 draw at The Dell in the second leg. But then we came up against Malcolm Allison's Sporting Lisbon in the next round and their approach was far more sophisticated than anything we normally encountered in the First Division. Sporting were on their way to a domestic league and cup double and they knew how to play in European competition. We didn't.

As usual we left ourselves open at the back, thundering forward in numbers at every opportunity, far too naive, far too gung-ho, lacking any kind of sense. Losing 4-2 at home, we were as good as dead for the return leg, which was creditably goalless, but the damage was irreparable and we came to the reluctant conclusion that for all our attacking flair we were just not the sort of side which thrived in Europe. But at least our seventh place in the league guaranteed us another shot the next season and, as it turned out, it was not a pleasant or profitable experience.

Talking of profits, the club had lost around £200,000 over the previous season, and money was tight. There were no Russian benefactors or self-made, ego-tripping billionaires running clubs in those days. Boards of directors were made up of local businessmen and professionals, in our case accountants and solicitors and they didn't like debt. Lawrie, who had grown used to fashioning sides on slender resources, was obliged to be prudent in the transfer market, selling Graham Baker to Manchester City for £225,000 and placating worried fans by bringing in Peter Shilton, at the time one of the best goalkeepers in the world. But there was a huge furore when Keegan quit just before the season started, taking advantage of a clause in his contract which allowed him to leave if he wanted to go, and he did.

Without any money to talk of, Lawrie replaced Keegan with Justin Fashanu on loan from Nottingham Forest and our fans were less than pleased. Many claimed to have bought season tickets in the belief that Keegan would be heading our challenge again. And Fashanu wasn't Keegan. In fairness, Kevin was irreplaceable. It didn't help that big Justin was lacking in skill and pace but he played with great honesty and endeavour and won over fans with his commitment. Knowing that he was taking over from one of the game's post-war legends must have been daunting but Justin was convivial company, full of life and by no means overawed by his task.

I think within football, if not the outside world, it was known that Justin was gay – the only one I ever knew about in football incidentally – but at that stage he seemed to be coping comfortably enough and it didn't matter to us so it was sad a few years later to learn he had taken his own life in such miserable circumstances.

Three months into this traumatic season, 1982/83, we lost Alan Ball, the third of our big names to leave us almost in as many months. Bally was 37 and was finding the pace of the First Division a little too much by this time. We all warmed to Alan as a player and as a person. His attitude was always perfect in that he trained superbly, to the maximum of his ability, but knew how to enjoy himself. He loved a bet, loved a drink, but it never got in the way of his performance and, as a World Cup winner, he played with great pride to his final appearance. When Bally spoke in that much-impersonated high-pitched trill, everybody listened because he knew what he was talking about. He could be very funny and carried with him a charisma that matched Keegan's. The best way to describe him socially was as the life and soul of a party and he liked nothing better than to get on a microphone and belt out

'New York, New York' or another Sinatra standard, 'My Way', all delivered in a surprisingly deep voice.

Not surprisingly we made a poor start to the season, struggling to recover from all the off-field problems and after losing to Liverpool and Tottenham we were bottom of the table before recovering to finish an unflattering 12th.

The season however will be remembered mainly for the infamous UEFA Cup match in Sweden in the little-known town of Norrkoping. It became known as the rape that never was. As usual I slept through it all. The night after we had been eliminated by the local team, Dennis Rofe, with whom I had been rooming, and I came down for our breakfast and the place was buzzing with whispers. A girl was alleging she had been raped by two Southampton players and the police were now involved. Alan Woodford, a solicitor and the club chairman, was taking statements from each of us as to where we had been after the match. When we got to the airport to go home we had to endure an identity parade and the girl picked out Moran and Wright. We flew off as they headed for the cells and it was some weeks before Moran was freed after the allegations against him had proved to be completely unfounded.

The loss in football terms of Moran was considerable and we only started to revive when Mick Mills brought his calming influence and efficiency to our defence, another major coup for Lawrie incidentally, bringing experience to a team which contained, now that the big three had gone, some great potential in Moran, Danny Wallace, Wright and Reuben Agboola. Moran showed how much we had missed him with a hat-trick against Manchester City and Wallace ended as our leading scorer that season with 12, making it clear that here was a Saints youth product snatched from under the noses of the London clubs ready to make a big impression. We now know that his move to Manchester United didn't quite work out and that he contracted multiple sclerosis and there is evidence to suggest that the onset of his illness contributed to his decline so he was never able to fulfil his great promise.

Danny was often my room-mate and I was something of a mentor to him in his early days, talking him through matches, using my experience to guide his searing pace. Danny at that stage had this great upper body strength, which enabled him to jump far higher than a man of 5ft 5ins should be expected to. Lawrie devised a system to exploit that pace and skill so that we always played with three up front to get on the end of his crosses. It made for great attacking football. I used to tell Danny I would put the ball behind the opposition's left-back for him to run on to, as a springboard from defence. It worked time and again. Incidentally, I always felt his younger brother Rodney was every bit as good.

Mark Wright was rapidly becoming an important player for us and attracting attention from bigger First Division clubs and was not far away from earning the first of his 45 England caps. It was no more than he deserved because the great qualities first identified were now being augmented by experience and he must have been a formidable opponent. Likewise Steve Williams, a lad from Romford, who had escaped the attention of all the London clubs as Wallace had and learned his craft in Southampton's youth system. The midfield with Ball alongside him and Nick Holmes and myself was as strong as any in the league and one of the reasons why Lawrie was able gradually to overcome the loss of his star names.

Williams earned five England caps and was sold to Arsenal for £600,000 later but just because he and Wright were young and had not cost us any decent money didn't mean they were content to go about their business subserviently. They were both strong characters and not afraid to voice their opinions or, as it turned out, be prepared to accept orders blindly. This didn't always sit well with Lawrie who, with his military background, was not used to insubordination in the ranks.

There were occasions when the two of them, not necessarily together, would argue with Lawrie and the coaches and it was clear the manager didn't like his authority being questioned. During one heated half-time inquest, I went into the shower and toilet room when Wright and McMenemy came in and started a scuffle and a fight. Lawrie, of course, was an imposing figure, but Wright was just as tall and wasn't being brow-beaten. Before I knew what was happening there was some shoving and Wright pushed Lawrie into the water. From that moment, though they tolerated each other because they had to, relations were uneasy. Wright later went on to play for Derby and Liverpool and enjoyed a hugely successful career but Lawrie had much more trouble with him and Williams in terms of them being opinionated than he ever did with Keegan, Channon and Ball who, for all their individuality, always knew where the ultimate authority lay.

We fared only moderately in the cups, losing to a weakened Tottenham in the FA Cup and reaching the fourth round of what was then known as the Milk Cup before being beaten by Manchester United. It says much for Lawrie, though, that he used this transitional season as a springboard for what must still be regarded as the club's best season in 1983/84. That took a lot of skill, planning and some judicious signings over the summer of 1983 and during the season. We could have gone the other way entirely. Our critics would have noted our decline, the loss of key players and the apparent failure to replace them. But Lawrie, within the confines of his budget, brought in the much-travelled maverick Frank Worthington, and later left-back Mark Dennis, whose disciplinary record Birmingham had decided made him too hot to handle, plus Alan Curtis, a Welsh international striker from Swansea. None of them would have been the sort of players clubs like Liverpool, Manchester United and Arsenal might have wanted but Lawrie knew what he was doing.

Not many managers would have been able to blend the young players coming through the system with one or two like Worthington and Mills at the tail-end of his career and adding them to the established players such as Williams, Shilton, Holmes and myself to form a team which came within a whisker of glory. But Lawrie did.

At the basis of it all was his idea to adopt a 3-4-3 system, a formation unfamiliar in England but which suited us as a team and the players contained within it. There was no better keeper than Shilton at the time and his presence tended to intimidate the opposition because he could give that impression of being unbeatable.

Key to making it work was Agboola in the sweeper role, a swift and adaptable young Londoner who had again come through Lawrie's youth system to hold down a regular place behind a defence which had Mills and Dennis pushing up from full-back into midfield and Mark Wright a significant figure in the heart of our resistance. In midfield we had Williams, Holmes and myself, all seasoned campaigners, plus the overlapping full-backs, and up front there was Worthington, Moran and Wallace to choose from. Moran and Wallace were full of goals, as was the whole team, getting between us 79 in league and cups.

To put all this together Lawrie and his staff had to make sure the players concerned fitted the roles being designated to them. It was a system in which we all knew exactly what we had to do. As a result, anyone connected to the club, not least the fans, will remember 1983/84 with lasting affection. For this there is really only one architect and that's why, to return to my theme, I'm still perplexed all these years later that Lawrie McMenemy has not been given his proper due. Every club has its heroes, Southampton more than most in many ways, but it seems they have forgotten the great moderniser, the man who made a team everyone wanted to play for.

Southampton once had a reputation for managerial loyalty few could match. I am told that when Lawrie eventually left in 1984 he had been only their fifth manager since the Second World War, the little matter of 38 years. A few years later they were changing managers with the frequency others change their socks. They could have done with someone of Lawrie's authority, discipline and foresight during those turbulent times.

One day I would like to think the club will realise just what he achieved and find some way of acknowledging it at the stadium or in some other form. I never came across a player who didn't like playing for him. Yes, there were the occasional rows and arguments but those happen at every club. In my view the way he kept the team evolving was a managerial masterclass and Southampton Football Club should recognise how important he was to them.

11

So Close To The Double

F OR SOUTHAMPTON to have achieved the coveted league and FA Cup double as we so nearly did in 1983/84 would have been an incredible achievement for a provincial club with money as limited as ours. Tottenham had done it in 1961, Arsenal had done it in 1971 and now Manchester United and Chelsea have done it but these were big clubs who could afford to bring in the world's best players. Yet we came within a couple of results of joining a small and very illustrious club of double winners. In the end we were runners-up to Liverpool in the First Division by three points and beaten in extra time in an FA Cup semi by Everton. In each case we were a tiny margin from history.

In my view we were never likely to overhaul Liverpool as league champions but we should have won the Cup and to have got so close was heartbreaking, all the more so after what we went through. The record books show we only used 21 players in the league, played in 51 matches and scored 79 goals in total but what they don't show is that we did it with a swagger, with

162

flair and a smile. The days of Channon, Keegan and Ball may have been by now a distant memory but their legacy was a free-flowing style and a commitment to attack and entertain.

In many ways this was the peak of my career in that I was Southampton's Player of the Year, scoring 19 league and cup goals from midfield. My reward, such as it was, came with my final international appearance at Wrexham in May 1984 on the basis, I like to think, that England couldn't ignore my league form or Southampton's success. After that 1-0 defeat by Wales, I was of course ignored for ever.

I played in all 51 matches as usual. I say as usual because I had managed to avoid injuries to that point and I still loved playing in an enthusiastic, almost child-like way. I just enjoyed being out there in front of big crowds and pitting my skills against the best players and in that respect I was so lucky because there were (and probably still are) a surprising number of professionals who don't always feel the same way. For me it was never a chore, never a job to pay the bills, even though in my position there were a lot of bills to pay.

For me the greatest accolade in any season is always being named Player of the Year because the decision is made by the fans in terms of votes and to have pleased them, moved them sufficiently to indicate me as the most consistent performer, was a great privilege and gave me a big lift. Not only was I at a career high, I think the same might be said of Steve Moran, our mobile and pacy striker, who got 25 goals over the season and was as good as any striker in the country at that point. Steve's problem was a recurring back injury so although in terms of appearances he had a full career with us, Leicester, Reading, Exeter and Hull he never played for England beyond a couple of caps at Under-21 level and didn't quite fulfil his potential. Danny Wallace got some great goals that season and with Worthington still a high-class target man, we must have been a difficult side to play against.

No match among the 51 mattered more or stood as much as our FA Cup trip to Fratton Park, that cauldron of anti-Southampton hatred. We didn't play each other often which made the occasion still more important. We were by the time the fourth round came upon us contenders for the First Division championship, Portsmouth were mid-table in the Second Division, but the Cup has a habit of cutting gaps in class and the muddy, heavy pitch further reduced any advantage we might have had.

I had played in plenty of North-East derbies and every one of them was fiercely fought but the build-up to this one was more intense than I had expected with an edge to it that was a little more sinister than those I had left behind at Middlesbrough. Fratton Park can be an intimidating place for the unwary but Lawrie made it perfectly clear that there was more than a fleeting bit of local prestige at stake and for the best part of 90 minutes there was precious little in it. We knew it was going to be tough and it was. Pompey fans threw coins at us, banana skins, all kinds of bits and pieces so you took your life into your hands if you got too near them on the touchline. We needed every ounce of our First Division experience to keep Portsmouth – and their supporters – at bay and if their bouncy little front-runner Alan Biley, the man with the Rod Stewart haircut, had taken his chances, who knows what might have happened.

The noise from the crowd was unbelievable, deafening almost, and as the match drifted towards its conclusion foremost in Southampton minds was how to get off the pitch at the final whistle without being molested. But deep into stoppage time we fashioned a winner out of nothing in a quite extraordinary sequence of events. Mark Dennis took a throw-in, Frank Worthington helped it on to me with his weaker right foot to my 'foreign' area at inside-right. With my right foot, the wrong one in my case, I played what turned out to be a perfect ball to Moran who volleyed home with his left foot which was by no means the one he favoured. It was the main game on *Match of the Day* that night and I think it might only have been then that we realised how the goal had come about.

With seconds left of course there was no way back for Pompey whose fans had been silenced for the only time in a tempestuous afternoon and when the final whistle went there was a fresh hail of objects hurled at us from the terraces. We milked it, running over to our fans and smirking at those in blue and white. As their dejected fans trudged off into the late afternoon gloom, Danny Wallace and Steve Williams went round picking up the coins which had so narrowly missed us and came back to the dressing room with a bonus of £3.50 plus a few bits of fruit. Lawrie joked about our post-match haul on television and in the papers afterwards but it was no laughing matter for those of us who had to play in the game and I doubt if Moran, who scored 99 goals for Southampton, ever got one that was more important. As my team-mates got on the police-escorted coach hoping the windows wouldn't come crashing in, I headed to the airport in a bid to see my daughter. That's how my life was at the time.

Having beaten Nottingham Forest in the third round, Portsmouth in the fourth and Blackburn in the fifth, we cruised into the semi-final by virtue of beating Sheffield Wednesday 5-1 in a quarter-final replay. I think we really fancied our chances of beating Everton in the semi at Highbury. We had lost to them 1-0 at Goodison Park not long before but, like most clubs, they were strong at home and we felt that we had the measure of them since there was nothing about them we feared. They were hard-working, busy but orthodox and on neutral territory we thought our pace might be a deciding factor. We were bang in form, knew exactly what to expect and were well prepared. One more win and we would be at Wembley.

The key to our strategy was getting Steve Williams fit. In the build-up to this game all the talk was of our play maker, an important player for us but who had been struggling with injury for some time. Steve wanted to play but he wasn't 100 per cent, not anywhere near it in fact. Lawrie had a big decision to make and in the end he thought the risk was worth taking. Had this been a league match, Williams would not have played but this was a one-off and we were all glad to see his name on the team sheet. Sadly, it didn't work out. Williams was well off the pace and was nowhere near the imposing player we knew him to be.

Even so in my opinion we were by far the better team and I seem to recall Neville Southall, one of the best goalkeepers in the country at the time, making half a dozen outrageously good world-class saves to deny us the goals we deserved. The match drifted into extra time and still we firmly believed we would prevail. Then with three minutes left, little Adrian Heath, the smallest player on the pitch, headed the Everton winner. I never felt so deflated on a football pitch or so low. Had we been seen off by the better team we would have held up our hands and acknowledged it. But we came away from Highbury feeling like we had been mugged, deprived of a place at Wembley by a team who on the day had been saved by the magnificence of their goalkeeper. It was one of the most frustrating days of my professional life and at 29 I feared my chances of a Wembley final had gone forever although they hadn't, as it turned out.

Maureen and I went off that night to meet our friends at Camberley where I did my best to blot out the disappointments of the afternoon, but while they, thankfully, weren't much interested in the outcome of a football match, in quiet moments my mind wandered back to Highbury. As if to emphasise our failure we were obliged through a quirk in the fixture list to play Everton at The Dell three days later in a First Division match and we won easily, 3-1, with me scoring twice. Revenge yes, but to Everton went the end-of-season prestige of an FA Cup Final appearance against Manchester United.

The final league table of that season shows how close we came to winning the championship but in truth I don't think it was ever likely. In those days it was still two points for a win and Liverpool were a fantastically strong side at the time and always just about in control of their destiny. We never were. What made it exciting for us was a superb late run of six wins and three draws from the last nine matches, starting with that victory over Everton and followed by another over West Ham at home a few days later.

One of the more significant results was an 8-2 thrashing of Coventry in which Wallace and Moran each got hat-tricks after I had got the first, but it was always a forlorn hope because experienced Liverpool showed no signs of wilting under the pressure of being leaders. I got two more in a 5-0 thrashing of what I believe was a depleted and weakened Tottenham side at The Dell and we finished with breathless away wins at West Bromwich and Notts County.

It wasn't enough. Liverpool were always just tantalisingly out of reach but if there was one result which stood out above all others as the reason for us not getting even closer it was us losing 2-0 at home to Notts County in November. Notts County were relegated at the end of the season and beating us was one of their better results, but it was a costly setback which at the time left us trailing in ninth and made our late-season surge all the harder to maintain. Who says results from early in the season are not important? They all are.

The end of my three-year contract was looming and bearing in mind my dire financial position I needed to improve my £35,000 a year at Southampton or go somewhere where I would get a wage which would allow me to cope far better with my unusual domestic situation. I was in a good position to negotiate in many respects although I had no agent to help me. No one did in those days. We had to do our own contract negotiations and I was aware I had never been especially successful in my previous dealings.

You will recall how, having signed for Southampton in the first place, I came away feeling that I might have done better in money terms, made Southampton sweat a bit, seen who else might have been interested in me. Instead, I found out about the possibility of joining them in the morning and signed by nightfall. But here in the summer of 1984 I was in a much stronger position. We had just come within a few goals of winning the double, I was a current international (just about) and at 29 I still had plenty more good years in me, or so I thought. If Saints didn't think of offering me a substantial pay rise I could surely find a top club who would. If I had been in that position now my agent would either have driven a hard bargain with Southampton or hawked me around our rivals to see if any of them might have been interested. I would also at my age have been able to move on a free transfer. This was pre-Bosman and Southampton could have expected to receive a transfer fee way in excess of the £600,000 they had paid for me.

There was also a reluctance on my part to move my family again. Having brought them all the way to the South Coast three years before and started afresh in such difficult circumstances I didn't want to do it all again so soon, if at all. Had I joined a club less geographically isolated it might have been possible to change employers without the upheaval that goes with it. But even if I had transferred to a London club, the nearest metropolitan area, it would have meant a round trip each day of 140 miles or so for training and matches and anywhere else was out of bounds unless we sold up and moved.

In any case why would I have wanted to leave Southampton in 1984? We were one of the best teams in the league, there was Europe to look forward to again, a solid core of experienced players and some great youngsters coming through Lawrie's youth system. In footballing terms there were not many clubs I could have joined in which my lot would have improved. So when Southampton offered me £50,000 a year for the next three years I was happy enough to sign the contract. I don't think I short-changed myself this time. It was about the going rate for a player in my position and I would have been the envy of those who didn't realise £15,000 of it was heading in the direction of my ex-wife's bank account every year. In contract terms I was in the strongest position I had ever been, a mixture of relative youth and copious experience, and I think I was conscious when agreeing terms that this was probably the last big pay day of my playing career.

Within a year I was beginning to regret what I had done, but that's another story, and at the time I had absolutely no regrets or second thoughts. I was committed now to Southampton until I was 32 and I was quite happy with my decision.

We should have kicked on in 1984/85 but a debilitating sense of disharmony crept into the club that stopped us building on our success of the previous season and mounting a serious challenge for the honours which had eluded us the year before. Maybe it had something to do with Lawrie's own sense of unease. Lawrie had enjoyed fantastic success and in his own way had become a commodity. He had been manager at The Dell for the best part of ten years and enjoyed a national profile. But for all the great players who had passed through his hands there was not a lot to show for it in terms of trophies and I suspect he had got to the stage when he thought he had taken the club as far as he could. Saints had been punching above their weight for years and when he looked at The Dell he was still looking at a stadium which didn't really belong in the First Division.

There was talk of him going to Manchester United as Ron Atkinson's replacement, a job to die for and one which would have provided the pinnacle to any man's career. But, for whatever reason, it didn't happen. Alex Ferguson took it and restored the club to the eminence of Matt Busby's time and bettered anything Busby had ever done. I wonder even now if Lawrie regrets not going to Old Trafford, regrets not making the big step up.

The result of him not going was that the club was never quite the same again while I was there. Lawrie was unsettled, perhaps thinking he had missed out, and as we know quit a year later in an ill-starred move to Sunderland.

On paper we had another good year, finishing fifth, but below the surface all was not well. Worthington became embroiled in a dispute over personal terms and moved on yet again, to Brighton, and later Williams and Wright spoke out in public against the manager, the man who had groomed them for stardom. But Lawrie was as canny as ever in the transfer market and brought back Joe Jordan from Italy as Worthington's replacement while rivals hesitated. Joe was something of a Scottish legend and brought with him a reputation for on-field nastiness, a stance which it pleased him to maintain. I first came across Joe when he was a junior at Leeds and I knew him as an exceptionally good target man, probably as good as any around at that time. Coming back from Verona, he had lost a little mobility but he was still a formidable footballer and as well as getting 12 league goals himself, he made a few for the grateful Moran. Without his teeth he frightened us almost as much as the opposition but underneath his public persona of intimidating hard man, he was a gentle, pleasant family-orientated man and good to have on our side.

So too was Shilton, not the easiest person to understand, but a reassuring figure behind our back four and without a doubt one of the reasons why our defence was always so strong. Shilts was not great on crosses, I'm not sure if many teams worked that one out, but much of our defensive work in training was aimed at preventing crosses coming into our box. In all other respects, he was exceptional, not least his shot-stopping, but when it came to crosses he could be indecisive and unsure and he relied heavily on Wright, in the main, to see off the aerial danger and allow him to stay on his line.

Shilts played every league game but, uncharacteristically, I missed a few with a broken toe, sustained in a goalless home draw with Hamburg in the first round of the UEFA Cup. I played through it, thinking I could overcome the pain, but it was sufficient to keep me out of the return leg in Germany where we lost 2-0, another European setback at a time when we had greater expectations.

All the while Lawrie seemed to be fretting, his team was showing unhappy signs of open revolt. Agboola, whose pace and reading of a game made him a natural sweeper, was exposed in a nightclub incident which hit the headlines and Lawrie, who didn't like such publicity, shipped him off to Sunderland at the first opportunity. But most damaging of all was when Wright and Williams, two by now mature and high-calibre footballers, came out openly about their disputes with the manager after one of our three, ultimately unsuccessful, Milk Cup matches with QPR. For the first time since Lawrie took control of the club he was being undermined and he had to do something about it. In a way it was odd that while he was able to cope with the egos of the superstars a few years earlier he was now being threatened by lads he had nurtured as teenagers.

His answer was to grant Williams a transfer, which allowed him to join Arsenal where I think it is fair to say he was never quite as influential as he had been with us. Wright lost his England place while all this was going on and yet what made these outbursts all the more peculiar was that they came at a time when we were going through a 14-match unbeaten run in the league. That ended with a 2-1 defeat at Coventry in

December and we had a rocky spell that month losing at home to Watford, Williams's last game, and Sheffield Wednesday. It certainly made training a bit different and it was a shock to see so much destructive activity going on within the club, so much unnecessary in-fighting, but Lawrie got us through it, all the while wrestling with his own doubts about his future.

As ever, he steadied the ship with another shrewd signing – how often have I said that? – replacing Williams with Jimmy Case. What a character. Jimmy made his name at Liverpool as a midfield tough guy, renowned for a ferocious shot and his equally ferocious tackling. As one of the few local lads in the Liverpool team, his reputation as a midfield enforcer meant his true ability wasn't always recognised and sometimes having so many star players in a great team detracted from his proper worth. Jimmy only ever got one England Under-21 cap but he came to the game late after completing his apprenticeship as an electrician and was eventually sold to Brighton in part-exchange for Mark Lawrenson.

At Brighton he played in the 1983 FA Cup Final and he came to us in March 1985, almost 31 and bought by Lawrie at a knock-down £30,000, many people believing his best days were behind him. How wrong they were because Jimmy gave us great service and was still playing in the lower divisions almost ten years later. It was not until you trained with people like Jimmy that you realised just how good they were, and with him as an example just how hard they could be. He had been brought up the Liverpool way, and it showed. The expression 'hard as nails' is a bit of a cliché but I can think of no better way to describe him or his attitude. Nothing frightened him, no opponent's reputation was too big.

What we quickly discovered was that there was more to Jimmy's game than his steel-trap tackling. He was an exceptional right-footed passer and a master tactician and with Williams long gone, Jimmy restored our midfield equilibrium, him on the right and me on the left at first although I think he came to play his best football for us in the centre of midfield in a holding role.

We used to practise our defending in training, using the younger lads as opponents and you could see then how some of them were a little wary of getting entangled with him. In matches, Jimmy was the great protector. Little Danny Wallace, because he was so fast and mobile, was a target for all kinds of intimidatory tactics from opponents, even those with big international backgrounds. Danny was not scared easily but he was the victim of some extraordinary tackling at times, aimed at slowing him down. Jimmy was having none of that. He would either go over a few minutes later and have a quiet word with the perpetrator or wait for an opportunity to show what a hard tackle really felt like.

Referees were always aware of him of course and he was no stranger to yellow and red cards but he had ways of getting his message across and his arrival at The Dell was a timely boost after the off-field uncertainty and got us through the season to a respectable conclusion. In fact we had qualified for Europe again, little knowing that soon after the end of the domestic season came the Heysel incident involving Jimmy's old club Liverpool in which 39 fans died, causing all English clubs to be banned from European competition the following year, an illogical UEFA decision which badly hit clubs like ours who had no history of violence at home or abroad. It is all the more of a shame because I felt we had just the right sort of balanced team to have made an impact in Europe at last. Had we been in Europe, maybe Lawrie would have stayed.

Jimmy was deaf in one ear and far from being a disadvantage, on the pitch he turned it to his advantage, pleading with referees that he had never heard their whistling and no referee wanted to be seen booking a player with a disability. But we all learned from Jimmy, even me to an extent, and for the younger players he would have been an educator. By the end of that season the fans had forgotten about Steve Williams. The only setback near the end of the season was a broken leg sustained by Wallace against Leicester but he had the summer to get over it, and he did.

At the end of the season we were booked to play a series of matches in Trinidad and Tobago and while that sounded like a bit of fun, it was carried out against a mood of unhappiness in the Southampton camp. The reason was Lawrie McMenemy. He was clearly beginning to think he was in the wrong place and, for the first time in four years, so did I. We may well have finished fifth but I think Lawrie had come to the conclusion that he needed a bigger stage. The Manchester United near miss had obviously played on his mind and I felt that if he went, as it appeared he wanted to, the club could only go backwards.

Just before we flew to the Caribbean I handed in a transfer request. There comes a time in a player's career when he knows that it's time to move and I had reached that stage. Lawrie wasn't pleased and we had a chat about it. I can remember his advice now. 'Don't leave. Think about it over the summer. Don't do anything rash.' So we went to Trinidad with nothing much resolved but with a general feeling that something had to happen. On our itinerary was a match against Manchester United, still not then the power they are now, and we defeated them and I always felt that if we had beaten Everton in that semi-final the year before we would have also beaten United. I just think their style at the time suited us.

But things were brewing behind the scenes while we were in Trinidad although we didn't quite know what until the lads stumbled on some English newspapers, probably a day or two old. Imagine our collective response to the news all across the back pages of Lawrie McMenemy on the point of going to Sunderland. It was a shock, no other word, because nothing had been said about it beforehand and it left us individually wondering where we stood in the grand scheme of things. I thought back to the way Lawrie had told me not to leave the club just a few days before we flew out. All the while he must have been planning to do exactly the same thing himself. Sunderland were a big club with a big following, bigger than us but not any more successful. As a Geordie, perhaps Lawrie felt he could introduce the formula he had perfected at Southampton, aligning older players who had been discarded elsewhere a little before their time with young lads coming through the system, to turn them into the giants of the North-East, and this time he was ready to give it a try.

So where did that leave us? Worried for the future, mystified and, in my case, wondering why he had told me to stay when he was, in effect, packing his bags. As Lawrie departed, all kinds of names were being touted as his replacement. Any manager would have relished the chance to continue Lawrie's work at a club as stable as ours. In those days we didn't sack our managers. They stayed a long time, as long as they wanted, and the board of directors, gentleman professionals to a man, craved only smooth continuity.

There must have been a long list of high-grade applicants so I'm not sure we were best pleased when it was announced that Chris Nicholl would be returning from Grimsby. I respected Chris as a player but I was not alone among the players in thinking we could have done far better. Still unsure about my future, I thought the board had played safe in appointing Chris, maybe because they feared the unknown. As I deliberated my future I was playing golf at Dunwood Manor when I was approached by Ted Bates, who must have been influential in Nicholl's appointment, who took me aside to plead with me to stay.

'We want to make you captain next season, you are a vital part of the team. Please don't go,' Bates said. He wanted me to assist Nicholl's settling-in period as the senior pro and, a year into a three-year contract, I opted to stay. I could see Matt Le Tissier and Alan Shearer coming through and I thought that with the right managerial backing, they could become outstanding Southampton players and I liked the thought of being captain. Even so, there was a part of me that couldn't help thinking that Lawrie McMenemy might help me fulfil a childhood ambition by signing me for Sunderland.

12

Southampton's Wrong Choice

W HY SOUTHAMPTON picked Chris Nicholl to replace Lawrie McMenemy I will never fully understand. Yes, it was the safe option, but he was not up to the job and he did well to last as many years as he did. It was only because Southampton had no history of sacking their managers that Chris was in charge for six seasons, in my opinion well beyond his true shelf life.

Chris was an English-born Northern Ireland international, a formidable defender who took a perverse pride in the number of times he had broken his nose playing football. His nose certainly bore the scars of many a battle and as a player you very much wanted him on your side. He was frightening to play against because he was hard in the tackle, strong in the air and rigidly disciplined. Whatever the occasion he gave 100 per cent and no opponent came off the pitch having had a comfortable afternoon. After playing for us at the end of a long and successful career which also included Aston Villa he left to learn about management and coaching at Grimsby, a good place to cut his teeth since the club had also produced McMenemy.

Maybe Saints' directors thought Chris was the next Lawrie, having served a similar apprenticeship, but things don't work like that in football. They were two very different people for a start. Where Lawrie enjoyed the media spotlight and spoke with fluency and style, Chris was introverted and suspicious. Where Lawrie was prepared to take chances with some of the game's biggest egos and reputations, Chris preferred to recruit from the lower divisions players he knew he could control.

In fairness to Chris, when he became manager in 1985, what we were not aware of at the time was that he had been told to cut the large wage bill he had inherited from Lawrie. It wasn't crippling in the way it damaged the club 20 years later but the parsimonious directorship could see the danger signs and told him it had to be reduced. That of course meant removing the star names and replacing them with cheaper alternatives, at the same time keeping Southampton in the First Division and competing with clubs who could afford to pay large salaries. Any manager would have found that difficult.

Having spent two years examining players in the third and fourth divisions he reckoned there were plenty of decent players there thirsting for a chance to step up. They would also not cost as much in wages. This was his theory and with some of the more expensive players getting on a bit in years, his task was always going to be difficult. The directors had at least given him a much-respected number two in Tony Barton, who had led Villa to European Cup glory, and I always found the softly-spoken Barton a much more sympathetic character and far easier to approach. In contrast, Chris struggled to get his ideas across and could be reluctant and withdrawn.

None of which made it easier for him to cope with some of the players Lawrie had left behind. Chief among those was the highly talented but personally erratic left-back Mark Dennis. The papers referred to him as 'Mad Mark' and 'Psycho' because he was always being sent off in the days when it was comparatively hard to get a red card, and his off-field escapades and domestic dramas were gleefully reported. Mark was a brilliant footballer and an amiable lad but he was not easy to handle and Chris had no clue how to do that in a fair and sensitive way.

Daft as a brush is an expression which comes to mind when talking about Mark, a real joker and a man without malice or deliberate ill-intention. Mark had a habit of not coming into training and some of his excuses didn't bear close scrutiny. Once or twice his car 'broke down' and one occasion he said he was lost. Poor old Chris had his hands full, trying to think of a way to get the best out of him and keep him in check and disciplined. They were total opposites as people. Chris tried dropping him, telling the world he was injured, and trying to sell a player with his list of misdemeanours was always going to be extremely hard. As a result, we needed another left-back and before I knew it, Chris was asking me as club captain to do the team a favour by dropping back from my position as an attacking midfielder.

I couldn't refuse. But I wasn't happy either at being the fall-guy for Mark Dennis not being able to sort out his life and for the manager not being able to bring him into line. Over the next year or two I was being asked to play more and more in that position or as a sweeper and I felt I was being wasted. I prided myself as a professional footballer in being able to play any position on the pitch if required. Playing for Middlesbrough at West Bromwich on one occasion I was asked to go in goal when Jimmy Stewart went off injured. John Neal felt I could handle a ball and for 30 minutes I kept a clean sheet until such time as Stewart could come back after treatment. John Wile and Cyrille Regis, two outstanding headers of the ball, were against me and must have fancied their chances but I got away with it.

But back to Dennis. I may have been predominantly left-footed but I could have played anywhere on the right. I just felt that, while I could coast along at left-back, my strengths as a goalscoring midfield player were not being used. Opponents must have been pleased to see me back there, especially as I was not the best tackler.

Over the next year or so from his arrival in the summer of 1985, Chris allowed, or was forced to allow, Mark Wright, Andy Townsend and the last of our superstars, Peter Shilton, to move on and they were never adequately replaced. Even Mark Dennis went eventually in 1987, briefly to QPR and then Crystal Palace, the major part of his career over at 26.

Chris Nicholl's answer was to delve into the divisions outside the first, backing his judgement that some unfulfilled and undiscovered talent lay there waiting to be unearthed. The best of those that he brought to Southampton was Glenn Cockerill, a busy and determined midfield player from Sheffield United, but some of his other recruits were not consistently up to it. Gerry Forrest from Rotherham was a good right-back and wasn't the worst of his signings by any means but like a lot of players coming into the top flight at an advanced football age, he lacked a little self-belief and confidence. In effect he was replacing Mick Mills, who had left in 1985, and it wasn't fair to expect a guy with his background to fill the boots of a former England captain.

Others like Gordon Hobson, who followed Chris from Grimsby eventually, were out of their depth although he did get a few goals. The problem for us all, particularly the manager, was that Southampton crowds had grown used to seeing the best and as players we had grown used to playing with the best. So to see someone like Hobson up against high-class defenders every week was frustrating and worrying. In the two years I spent with Chris as manager it became increasingly clear that we were bringing in second-rate players and those of us left from Lawrie's regime grew to be unhappy and unsettled.

The first statement he made to us as the new manager of Southampton contained the phrase 'I'm not Lawrie McMenemy', which soon became apparent, and, 'I'm not a pretty face because I always gave everything for the team. You must all give 100 per cent in the same way.' Devoid of charisma or any kind of public relations acumen, the new gaffer struggled from the start to get his ideas across to the players.

There was one wonderful story to illustrate the confusion and lack of coherence in training when Chris decided we should play a game of shadow football in which we were playing 'against' no one, a simulation ploy aimed at getting us to be thinking about the way we played. Colin Clarke was with us by then. Clarke kicked off, passed the ball to Hobson, Hobson to Case, Case to Francis Benali and Benali back to goalkeeper Tim Flowers. The problem was Flowers was putting his cap in the net and didn't anticipate the Benali pass so the ball trickled over the line into the goal. One-nil down against no one. It took us a further 30 minutes to 'equalise'. The writing was firmly on the wall. Chris, a deep thinker who kept a lot to himself, quietly despaired.

At least there was Barton. We all spoke to him more than we did to Chris because he knew how to handle players, which Chris did not. Management is an art and Lawrie, for one, and Barton, for another, understood that every player was different and that some of us had problems away from the training ground. Mine certainly hadn't disappeared and there was always Mark Dennis lurking in the background like a needy child.

We still had some good players aboard when 1985/86 kicked off. Shilton was still first choice, Townsend, Case, Wright and Kevin Bond were there, Nick Holmes, Steve

Moran, Joe Jordan and Danny Wallace were still around and, before my conversion to defence, I played in all but one game, scoring 15 league and cup goals to make Nicholl's decision later to withdraw me from an attacking position all the odder in my estimation.

It was Southampton's centenary season so it was an additional honour to be captain at such a landmark but in truth the club was in a state of flux and never more was this evident than in our opening six winless matches, four of them lost. The club was coming to terms with Chris Nicholl who in turn was coming to terms with his new team. It was not a pleasant introduction.

Cockerill was Chris's first big signing and he made his debut on Luton's notorious plastic pitch where we were walloped 7-0. Playing on artificial surfaces is difficult at the best of times, requiring an adjustment, but on the day we were lucky it was only seven. At the end of the game the manager was a rattled man. I had planned to make the short trip from Luton to Heathrow to catch a flight to the North-East to visit my daughter but Chris put a stop to that. 'You're coming back with us because we're having a meeting at The Dell on Sunday morning,' he told me. I had no choice but to obey.

Glenn Cockerill took a lot of stick from fans in that game, although it wasn't his fault by any means. Glenn went on to prove himself a good player but throughout my time at the club with him he was the butt of abuse because the supporters saw him as Mr Average, which shows how spoilt they had been over the previous decade.

Luckily we had a mid-season revival, culminating in a 3-1 win over Brian Clough's Nottingham Forest in the last home match of the year in which I had the satisfaction of scoring twice. Our away form was poor all season and in the end we were grateful to finish 14th, not the sort of position Southampton were used to, and there was a nasty sting in the tail. Keith Granger only ever made two league appearances in his entire career but he will be remembered by Saints followers for letting in 11 goals. He shouldn't even have been playing because he was our third choice behind Shilton and Phil Kite.

Kite had dislocated his shoulder in training and as we came to board the coach for Everton, newly crowned as league champions, it was announced that Shilton would not be joining us because he was unwell. Keith, our youth team goalkeeper and not ready for this sort of occasion, was hastily drafted in to the team as rumours circulated about the reason for Shilton being 'unwell'. If he knew, Chris was not telling us. But the reason was bound to emerge eventually among the players and it did – Peter had been on a 'bender'.

Nothing went right for us at Goodison Park in his considerable absence with Peter Willis, a referee I knew well from the North-East, refusing to change his mind after allowing a Derek Mountfield goal to stand although the Everton defender had clearly used a hand. Keith's confidence ebbed from that very moment and 6-1 let us off a bit lightly. Shilton was still 'unwell' two days later when we ended our season at White Hart Lane and were on the wrong end of a 5-3 thrashing. As for Keith, I'm not sure he was ever the same goalkeeper, so traumatic had the drubbings been for him.

Our saving grace was the FA Cup. The draw for the third round is always eagerly awaited and imagine my pleasure when we were drawn to play Middlesbrough in the third round at Ayresome Park. I hadn't been back much since moving south but there were still some familiar faces among the stewards and backroom staff who were keen to be reacquainted with me even though we beat them. The reception was as hospitable as ever but the team was not the Middlesbrough I remembered and cherished and we won 3-1 with a hat-trick from Wallace.

Wigan were our fourth round opponents and it was a particularly good match for me in winning 3-0, Cockerill getting the first from my corner and then I added two more, the second of which came from a rebound after my penalty had been saved.

Millwall made life difficult for us in the fifth round. We needed two matches and penalties to see them off in the Milk Cup and they were no easier to put away here in the FA Cup. It was goalless at The Dell and Wallace got the only goal in the replay at The Den. Brighton at the Goldstone in the quarter-finals was straightforward enough, a 2-0 win, leaving us to play Liverpool in the semi at White Hart Lane.

There was, of course, great excitement in the city at the prospect of Wembley being only one match away and rightly so. But we were never going to win this one and for that I must blame Chris Nicholl and his team selection. We had our bad luck, I can't dispute that, but we made life difficult for ourselves long before the kick-off. There was nothing Chris could have done about Wallace's injury, sustained at Brighton, and then Mark Wright broke his leg during the match but we didn't help ourselves either.

If Liverpool had a weakness at the time it was in the air at the back and we still possessed in Jordan one of the best headers in the game, just the man to exploit it as long as we could supply the crosses into the box for him to attack. It was an obvious tactic, certainly, and no doubt Liverpool were mindful of the threat Jordan would pose. Wallace did play, without being anywhere near his best, but Jordan didn't. For some unknown reason and to our great surprise, Chris dropped him, a decision which must have delighted Liverpool when they saw our team sheet half an hour before the kick-off. You would have to ask Chris why he did this, ask him what he thought would be gained from leaving out our biggest threat. He might say that Joe had only played spasmodically and had not yet scored a goal but Joe thrived on the big occasion, knowing that in his declining football years this was a challenge to be met.

Losing Wright in a collision with Shilton and Craig Johnston was obviously a major setback at 0-0 but who did Chris ask to fill in his place in central defence? Me. I said I was versatile but at 5ft 7ins I was nobody's idea of a towering centre-half and of all the people asked to replace Wright I would have thought I was the last. More to the point, we had therefore lost another attacker by me being withdrawn so that we had no option but to sit back and invite Liverpool to attack us, hoping forlornly to hit them on the break.

Bond made a mistake in extra time to let in Ian Rush but in winning 2-0 Liverpool were always the better team. We lost because we put the wrong team on to the pitch and got what we deserved. For Chris Nicholl, reaching a semi-final in his first season of top level management was something to put on his CV but as the season drew to a close he was presiding over an increasingly unhappy camp, although I don't think he knew it. A lot of players no longer wanted to play for Southampton, the residue of the team Lawrie left behind were either coming to the end naturally or wanted to get away to further their careers. All the while Chris was looking for ways of removing the more expensive players because our wages were considered too high.

I was among those. I may have been captain but if he could have sold me, he would, of that I'm sure. I had a year left on my contract at this stage but I began to wonder what might happen after that. I thought to myself, what's best for David Armstrong? I was on a good salary, Maureen and the children were happily settled in the south and, for all the problems we left behind in the North-East still prevalent, we had a contented and peaceful home life. The last thing I wanted to do was to disturb all this and move for its own sake just to get away from Nicholl and a declining team.

Two players kept Southampton safely in mid-table the following season, 1986/87. That is maybe a bit of an exaggeration because Matthew Le Tissier was not then the outstanding player he was to become in a few years' time. But the other one was testament to Chris's knowledge of the football in the lower divisions. From Bournemouth came Colin Clarke, a prodigious scorer in the Third Division who had impressed our manager during the World Cup finals in Mexico playing for Northern Ireland. Against world-class defenders he saw enough in the powerfully-built Clarke to suggest he might make the transition to the top level, and he did. Clarke announced his arrival with a hat-trick on his debut in a 5-1 win over QPR at The Dell and went on to get another later in the season against Newcastle, also at home.

Le Tissier, aged 18, showed his potential with another treble, against Leicester, and Hobson got a hat-trick against Manchester City. That makes it sound like we had a super season, but for all Clarke's 20 league goals we finished 12th and I don't look back on it with any particular affection. This was partly because of the injury I got in November when I collided with David Rocastle and partly because I ended it playing full-time at left-back.

I got only the one goal against Liverpool in September, my lowest season's tally since I was a kid at Middlesbrough, and I think I knew deep down it could well be my last at The Dell from quite early on.

The highlight was a two-legged semi-final in the Milk Cup against Liverpool, a draw at home followed by a 3-0 defeat at Anfield but there were many more low points. We actually lost only two of our last 13 league games, the majority after I had been converted to left-back, but I don't think anyone was deceived into thinking that this might be the start of a new career for me. I wasn't. In fact by the time I played in my 268th and final match for Southampton in May 1987 in a 1-1 draw with Coventry I was already in dispute with Nicholl and the club.

One or two stalwarts were on their way or had gone by the time all this took place. Jordan had moved on, Dennis was no longer being chosen and heading for QPR and then Nick Holmes played the last of his 444 matches for the club in February.

I began to feel a bit isolated. Nick was a fantastic club man, an animal on the left side of the pitch, quiet and mild-mannered off it, and dedicated to the Southampton cause. If you had to select an example of how a professional should perform and behave you would choose Nick and there was never anyone fitter.

My problem with Southampton was monetary but was also about my pride, which was badly hurt. At the time of my injury no midfield player in the country had scored more goals, more regularly than me. Absolutely none. Yet 16 of my 22 league appearances that final season were spent at left-back, a job a young lad could have done just as well although Mark Dennis could have done it better than both of us. Mark had fallen out with the manager and was finished in his eyes but rather than buy a replacement, he put me in the number three shirt and told me to get on with it.

I used to say to Nicholl, 'The only way to win matches is to score goals. I have always been able to do that. Why keep me away from attacking positions?' But Chris had no real response because he struggled to express himself or to provide a rational reason for placing my square left peg in a round hole. It was illogical, unreasonable and in my view a waste of an experienced attacking midfield player. Lacking all kinds of managerial skills, the ability to keep everyone satisfied for as long as possible, all he did was make enemies. I felt abused, my loyalty taken for granted, as this ridiculous situation persisted until the bitter end, and it was a bitter end.

If he was worried about my fitness, he had no cause at that stage and I proved it on a post-season tour of Singapore where I played in every game without any physical reaction. All the time I was hoping the club would come up with some kind of financial offer to keep me for a seventh season and beyond, although I wouldn't have wanted to spend any more time than was necessary at left-back. When it came, I couldn't have been more disappointed. Chris took me aside, explained the financial problems the club were going through, which by then I knew about anyway, and then said he wanted me for next season on a pay-as-you-play basis on top of a small basic. This was his half-hearted effort to get me to sign a contract in which I would have dropped my salary by between £15,000 and £20,000 a year. I worked out that I couldn't have earned any more than about £35,000 at the very most and of course in my social predicament it was completely unacceptable.

It was a huge drop and Southampton obviously knew I would reject it, which I did. I believe I had reason to feel let down because I had given wholehearted service for six years, some of the best in the club's history, and my only injury blemish had been in that final season. Statistics were on my side. While I was out of the team in the middle of the season we had slipped into the relegation zone by the end of February but when I came back we picked up and went on that fine late run. Just a coincidence? Maybe.

To be honest, I found Southampton's attitude insulting and patronising. It would have been better if they had simply given me a free transfer and thanked me for my contribution. I would have been unhappy but I would have understood it and moved on. But to make an offer, which was so poor, expecting it to be rejected, was hard to fathom. If I had a history of injury frailty I would have seen their point of view, but 268 games in six years speaks of consistency and durability.

By turning down Southampton's offer I was available on a free transfer anyway but it was a sad and needlessly confrontational end to my otherwise very contented and sometimes thrilling career with the club. I don't know if it was Chris Nicholl's idea to make me that offer or if it came from higher. I think it was designed to make Saints look good in the eyes of their supporters. The club could say they had come up with a deal which I, as club captain, had turned down. It made me look like the culprit. Since neither the club nor I were ever going to make public the details it looked as if I had departed in a huff. I suppose in the light of what happened a few months later at Bournemouth they could say they were proved right, that I had a weakness, but until that injury at Exeter I had been doing fine.

So, out of principle, I quit Southampton with a heavy heart and a sense of grievance. I still thought I could play in the First Division and, as I had done at Middlesbrough, I had enjoyed a great relationship with the fans. For that reason alone, I considered I was being forced out with business unfinished. Here comes the irony. When I eventually signed for Bournemouth I agreed a contract which provided me with less money than Southampton had offered. But, as I say, there was a principle at stake and I couldn't see how I could ever work for Chris Nicholl again.

This was a shame because, for a start, I was looking forward to helping the young Matthew Le Tissier develop. Matt was my apprentice when he first came over from Guernsey, cleaning my boots, and you could see from day one that here was someone exceptional. He made his debut at 16 and in my last season he was just beginning to show the sort of qualities which should have won 50 England caps, not the paltry handful he got.

When it became clear various England managers from Terry Venables to Glenn Hoddle and Bobby Robson were suspicious of his 'laid-back' style, I was convinced he should go somewhere he would be better appreciated. There was a rumour that Michel Platini, then the French international manager, wanted him to play for France, which through his Channel Islands connection he could have done. I went to see him one day to get a ball signed and I told him that if I was in his position, with options available, I would defect to the French. They were among the best teams in the world at the time and he would have suited their style, as Platini must have realised. I think that with a bit of adjustment he could have become a big player for France and while he listened with respect to my argument, his heart was with England and they repaid him by ignoring him.

When you look at Matt's record in the Premier League there was a spell of a few years when no one got more goals consistently than Matt and it was not as though he was getting them while playing for one of the major clubs. Southampton owed him a massive debt for keeping them almost single-handedly in the Premier League for so many years and I'm not sure many other players could have done what he did. He was a fantastic, unfulfilled talent and I am amazed that those managers concerned never looked beyond that rather cumbersome, slow-footed approach and saw the way he would glide past defenders without appearing to accelerate before unleashing those magical long-distance shots. I would have thought he might have made a World Cup or European Championship squad or two just for his unrivalled ability to take penalties.

Did he suffer from staying with Saints too long? I think he should have tested himself with a bigger club, and I say that as a friend, but he loved the club and even after what they did to me at the end, so did I.

13

Preferring Bournemouth To Clough

BRIAN CLOUGH wanted me to join Nottingham Forest once it became clear my days as a Southampton player were over. I wasn't going to take a huge drop in pay. Chris Nicholl and the Saints board were in no mood to compromise either. So I had no option but to spend the summer of 1987 sat by the phone waiting to see where I might be spending the next year or two.

In fact Clough was among the last to get in touch and by then I had already made up my mind. I say Clough got in touch but he didn't actually do the dirty work. He left the negotiations to his assistant, Ronnie Fenton, but by the time we got to speak it had already been, thankfully, a hectic close season from my point of view. On the positive side I was still only 32 at the start of the summer with a wealth of top level experience so I didn't need to panic because I knew there would be interest once it had become known that I had left Southampton.

Agents were non-existent in those days or were the preserve of the very famous, so it was up to me to find a suitable club and to make sure I didn't sell myself short again. Every summer there is a long list of players either freed by their clubs as I had been or who were available for fees. It is uncertain and worrying for players because the time available to find new employment is short, perhaps the whole of June and half of July before teams report for pre-season training to prepare for the winter ahead. I felt I was better off than most because of my First Division background and pedigree but it didn't stop me feeling anxious. I did wonder if Middlesbrough might come in for me but that never happened and I had to be prepared to be patient.

I didn't have to fret for long. York City, then in the Third Division, wanted me to become their player-manager. The idea appealed to me greatly. As I had got older the prospect of becoming a manager became more and more of an ambition and having seen top class managers like Stan Anderson, Jack Charlton and Lawrie McMenemy at work, I believe I had learned a lot from them. I also thought I could do better than some other managers I had come across so to be offered this opportunity with an established and respected club was a potentially wonderful start to a managerial career. Denis Smith had just left the club and I travelled north to speak to Barry Swallow, then a director but previously a playing stalwart, about the vacancy. If all had been well, I would have taken it, but there was something not quite right as we spoke.

Barry was straightforward and made it clear there was no money pot for new players, but nor it seems was there any for me. When it got down to the cash side of the transaction I asked about a signing-on fee, a common enough occurrence in football and something I had assumed, wrongly as it turned out, would be offered to me. York had not even considered offering me a signing-on inducement even though it was clear they did want me to be their player-manager. Swallow said it wasn't possible and that was the end of our negotiations. A pity in many ways because it would have been a great place to start the management career I had planned for myself, but I was a little taken aback that they thought I would be prepared to step out of the First Division into the Third Division without any kind of compensation. As it happened, it was probably just as well that I didn't take the job because York had a poor season and were relegated and Bobby Saxton, who took over as manager, lasted only 15 months.

Then along came Sheffield Wednesday and Howard Wilkinson. They were in the First Division at the time and I liked the thought that I could play another year or two at that level. I was encouraged by their interest, Wilkinson told me of his plans and I happily signed an insurance form so that I could go with them on a pre-season tour of Germany. To that point I could see no reason not to join Wednesday other than social although we had not yet discussed the finer points of the financial side. I would have had to become a long-distance commuter because I wasn't going to uproot the family again. I suppose I would have gone north on a Monday morning and come home after matches on a Saturday, hardly ideal but it would only have been for a year or two and it was a small sacrifice to make for domestic harmony.

Wilkinson was credited with being one of the deep tactical thinkers of his generation and was well regarded by the FA and within the game generally, but I found him to be obsessed with fitness. Nothing else seemed to matter. Gary Owen, once of West Bromwich and Manchester City, was another trialist who came with us to Germany, but where he eventually signed, I didn't.

Getting to Germany, we slogged through six friendly matches in eight days in draining heat. At last we got a day off which Wilkinson described as 'a day of active rest'. This, I found out from his coach Peter Eustace, meant a five-mile run. I went to Wilkinson to find out if it was true and it was. 'Don't listen to what they tell you. You should speak to me,' he said. I responded by saying, 'You can book my plane ticket back home now because my body does not need these runs on top of six matches at my age.'

Wilkinson didn't make much effort to get me to change my mind although I had played soundly enough in the friendly matches. A Wednesday director drove me back to the airport and the move was well and truly off. I had no regrets at the time, other than I was now leaving it a bit late to find another club, at least one in the First Division. Wednesday did well enough without me, they finished 11th and took four points off Southampton, drawing at The Dell and winning at Hillsborough, which I might have enjoyed but I don't think I would have gained much from a year or two of the Wilkinson regime. There was nothing I saw in the week or two I had spent working with him which suggested anything special.

It was then I started to be seduced by the charms of Harry Redknapp. He had noted how, with much of the summer gone, I was still without a club and only a week or two away from getting the last of my Southampton pay packets. I would soon be officially without a club and, more importantly, without any money coming into the house. I was beginning to worry a bit now and Harry was reassuring and pleasant. We walked around those fields at the back of my house on a warm summer's day and talked and talked. Harry had a strong vision of his club's future and his own at its helm and from all points of view it seemed right. Bournemouth was just down the road, there was no need for the children to change schools and it appeared like a club going in the right direction.

As I say, Harry talked of getting into the First Division and I knew they already possessed some excellent players, among them David Puckett and Mark Whitlock whom I had known at The Dell. Harry liked to play in the manner he had grown up with at West Ham's famous academy under Ron Greenwood, which suited me, and there was no talk of pointless five-mile runs. The aim, Harry said, was to get out of the Second Division and I gave him my word I would sign for them. Deal done.

It was then that I got a call from Fenton who had replaced the legendary Peter Taylor as Clough's sidekick without having quite the same personality or the same impact in their time together. Even so, Fenton knew what he was talking about, said how highly Cloughie rated me and told me what sort of role he envisaged for me in the season ahead. I was excited by what he had to say and incredibly flattered that a man of Clough's distinction and eminence within the game should want me.

Clough was a one-off and a true maverick, the likes of which would probably not prosper or be tolerated in today's corporate-run football. His list of achievements at Derby and then Forest were incredible, not least winning the European Cup, and had he beaten Redknapp by a few days I would have felt it a privilege to join Forest. Had I joined them I would have been part of a team which finished third in the league and were beaten semi-finalists in the FA Cup. Instead I joined Bournemouth who finished 17th in the Second Division and spent much of the season avoiding relegation. Not that with my injury would I have played much part in that. But the point is I had given my word to Harry and while I had not actually signed anything and was technically a free agent, I am not the sort of person to go back on his word.

I am sure if I had rung him and told him Brian Clough had come calling he would have shrugged it off and gone looking elsewhere. Over his long career in management Harry would have won and lost players more distinguished than me. But I was happy with my decision and told a somewhat surprised Fenton that I was rejecting perennial honour-chasers Forest in favour of humble Bournemouth. In spite of all the things that happened subsequently in terms of the injury and my spells on the dole, I never regretted that choice. We can all look back on our lives and say 'what if' and had I joined Forest I might have stayed injury-free and played a couple more years in the First Division. But, then, I might not. In that respect I was just unlucky.

I only wish I had been able to repay Harry's faith. It all started well enough and with Whitlock in the same side we beat Sheffield United 1-0 on the opening day with the chaos and the misery which was to follow in a matter of weeks seeming impossible to imagine as I drove home that evening, very content in the belief I had chosen well. I got a penalty against Exeter in the Littlewoods Cup and goals against Bradford City and Birmingham but on 5 September my playing career was all but over.

I did try in vain to make a comeback but I knew in my heart of hearts it wasn't going to happen. There were substitute appearances against Manchester City, Stoke and Aston Villa five months later and I started my last game at Barnsley on 6 March, but I was struggling with pain all the time and I had to be replaced by an American, Brent Goulet. That was it. All that lay ahead was a grim series of operations and medical assessments and the second half of my life has been spent trying to maintain for Maureen and my family a standard of living they have a right to expect. At the same time I was being registered as partially disabled and was never again sure of regular employment. I have listed elsewhere my increasingly futile attempts to stay in football and instead had to come to terms with an endless series of outside jobs which have never given me lasting satisfaction or, of course, the same thrill or the same status.

Making that adjustment to 'civilian' life would have been much harder without the help of numerous kind people who had nothing, no reflected glory to gain from consorting with a limping ex-footballer but did so often out of the goodness of their hearts. Ian Butcher was one. There came a day when I realised I had to find a way beyond football to make a living. I was in my mid-30s, had children at school, a mortgage to pay and 30 years of working life ahead of me. But doing what if it wasn't football? Ian realised my predicament and briefly got me selling drinks for Silver Spring Soft Drinks and I must say I liked the idea of selling. I have always found it easy to talk to people and in many ways this was good therapy, having to go out among the public to make contacts and to persuade them to buy. I know many ex-footballers find it hard, harder than I did, to come to terms with the fact that nothing is going to be done for them any more in terms of life's basics, but although this particular job didn't last long I had discovered there was something else in life I was good at and selling is basically what I've done over the last 25 years in one form or another.

In 2002 another friend, Mervyn Houghton, asked me to work for him in Shamrock Quay, Southampton, selling office supplies, initially for three months, and office equipment has since been something of a speciality for me over the years, although, in vain at times, I did try other means of making a living.

Rob Whittington of Nurdin and Peacock Cash and Carry removed me from the dole but I just couldn't cope with the lifting of heavy cases of bottles and food because my ankle was not up to the task and I had to give it up. For a time I sold videos in Eastleigh, leasing them to the shops, but it was the office equipment business which almost put me back on my feet. Mervyn made me a full-time salesman and the business grew quickly when we got a contract supplying the American military bases in Britain. We even went to New York to make a presentation, a five-man band from Shamrock Quay, on Federal Plaza telling hard-to-impress American forces chiefs why they should buy our equipment. It was all a bit unreal.

From there we went to Washington to pitch for a contract supplying furniture and for the first time since I was propelled into retirement I felt I was on the up, the adrenaline was flowing as it had done when I was playing and I was undeniably a capable, persistent salesman. So much so that I was made a director by Mervyn in appreciation of my efforts.

I had also found a niche as a radio co-commentator at Southampton matches for a commercial radio station, Power FM, with the enthusiastic Peter Hood. This kept me in touch with the game and Southampton Football Club and I no longer felt quite as cut off from football in the way that I had been. Business was booming and we were even able to get Maureen in to look after the American business. She was quickly successful before suffering whiplash in a car accident.

Then it all started to go wrong, Mervyn wanted Maureen to go cold-calling and before I knew it I was on my way to work for Steve Taylor at A & A, another office equipment company, but things didn't quite work out there either. Working as a commentator meant that for most away matches, particularly in the north, I had to leave work on a Friday afternoon and A & A didn't like that. They put me on a three-day week for three years and the money Power FM paid me was never enough to compensate properly for the loss of two days' work. I left them eventually in August 2011 and went back on the dole, hopefully for the last time.

Luckily I knew a few people in the business by now and I approached Martin and Steve Shaw at ISL who were kind enough to take me on as an office equipment salesman and that's what I'm doing now. Maureen, by the way, is still involved in the same line, spending two or three days a week travelling to the American bases.

I like getting out and about, many loyal customers have come with me from company to company and I can make a living in cut-throat competition. I know I will never be the world's best salesman but I'm good at networking, building personal relationships, something I had to learn after football, and good at opening doors in a business sense. Yet nothing will ever replace football in my life. Nothing will ever adequately fill the gap.

What I miss most is the involvement of being with a professional club every day, the camaraderie, the humour, the fun. When it's gone there is suddenly a huge void. In my case I had no time to prepare for the loss, the bereavement. Older players can plan for the day when their legs can no longer carry them around the pitch like they used to. They can see younger players coming through, a generation different, and know their time is up. But I wasn't ready to go. I had been looking forward to another three years at least as a player and to have it taken away like that was desperately hard to take.

I knew a lot of people in football and always hoped there might be a way back in through them. My friend Bobby Hope got me doing some scouting for West Bromwich Albion but that didn't last. I tried ringing Alex McLeish numerous times when he was boss at Birmingham and Aston Villa but never got through, I never got a reply from Jim Magilton when he was at QPR and I'm still waiting for Alan Pardew to get back to me.

The tragedy from my point of view is that I still feel I have a lot to offer. I should be in the game in some capacity and I'm disappointed I'm not. Even the radio work, latterly covering Reading's matches, has dried up.

I hope I don't sound bitter, because I'm not. I was lucky to have played as long as I did, all those years in the First Division and for England. I was unlucky to have been injured when I was and for the injury to have such a lasting effect on my life and that of my family's. I like to think it's football's loss but I dare say other ex-players have said the same thing.

The problem is that you can quickly be forgotten. I recall one incident, which even now makes me angry, when I returned to Southampton, the club I had served for six years, to cover one of their matches against Doncaster for local radio. Thanks to my bald pate, I'm not unrecognisable and in fact I spend a lot of time saying hello to fans and officials whenever I do go back there. I like to think that when I return to both my old clubs I'm remembered with some affection and the reception I get usually indicates that. I say usually because on this occasion I was thrown out.

At St Mary's there is a large hospitality area which must hold 30 or 40 large tables for the many diners. It is known as the Mick Channon Lounge and on this particular day there were maybe only five or six tables being used. Two friends of mine, Bill Laidlaw and Steve Taylor, were hosting tables that day so I went in to shake a few hands and have a chat. As an ex-player I was doing a little bit of unpaid public relations for the club, talking about players and games from the past. As I was doing so I got a tap on the shoulder from a steward who told me firmly I had to leave. I thought it was a joke and waited for him to start laughing, perhaps even to ask for an autograph. But, no, he made it abundantly clear I had to get out. He never even asked if I had a ticket. I must have been in that particular lounge countless times and yet here I was, one of the club's few England internationals, being evicted.

My friends were outraged and embarrassed on my behalf and threatened to withdraw their custom, but the jobsworth won the day and I was out in the corridor before I knew it. Of course, this was a bit of a PR disaster since I went back to the press box where I was working and told them all about it. Needless to say, it reflected badly on the club when it got in the papers but it was a reminder, as if I needed reminding, that fame is transitory. I have never to this day received any kind of apology from the club.

Sometimes I have to laugh at the cruel tricks time plays. I went with some friends introduced to me by my pal Tony Bailey from a Birmingham-based company called Barton Storage to watch England play an evening match against Croatia not so long ago. After the game we went for a beer or two and a curry and we just about caught the last bus from Wembley to Ealing on the way to a hotel in Richmond where we were staying overnight. As we staggered up to the top deck and slumped breathlessly into our seats we joked about my change in fortune. A few years previously I was being escorted in and out of Wembley as an England international. Now I was hobbling as fast as I was able to catch the last bus away from the stadium.

It wasn't the only time I had been forced to laugh at myself. Frank Skinner and David Baddiel had a TV programme called *Fantasy Football League*, an off-beat look at the game, and I was a guest once or twice. Noticing my thickening girth, they made a ball out of me, a ball I later auctioned for charity at a dinner event I had organised.

Luckily, through it all, good and bad, my wife and children have stood by me. The arrival of Kate, our daughter and a sister for Justin and Christian, in February 1983, born in Winchester, was a godsend and completed us as a family. After what we had all been through she made a huge difference to our lives and our perspective. The boys idolise her and dote on her and speaking as her proud dad I have to say she has inherited her mother's lovely nature and goodwill towards those around her.

She was only in her first year at secondary school when she stood up on the bus and shouted down those among her pals who were cruelly laughing at a disabled child in her class and she has always maintained that sense of justice and fair play. She lives with Dylan, a Saints season ticket holder who is old enough to remember a portly number ten called Armstrong in red and white stripes.

We had a family expedition to India in 2008 for Christian's marriage to Poonima, a Hindu wedding performed only when the stars were right and which lasted a memorable week. Christian had been working in Delhi when he came across Nicky, as she is now known, working in Debenhams there. The stars being right meant the ceremony was performed at 4.30am, although we were obliged to be in place by 8pm the previous night but it was worth the wait and the stars have been proved absolutely correct.

We did all the tourist things including visiting the Taj Mahal and Chris's dad, Howard, happily joined us. Several of our friends came too, including Bertie and Sheila, but the trip had its tragic side. Bill Laidlaw complained of breathlessness going up some stairs during the week-long celebrations and we had to take him to a hospital after a visit to the Golden Triangle. Bill was eventually diagnosed with leukaemia and died two years later aged 62.

Nicky's parents needed convincing we were all behind the marriage, which of course we were, but they must have wondered about our government since she has struggled, even with their baby Asha Lily, to get a visa to get into Britain even though she married a United Kingdom citizen. She paid the penalty for abusers of the system but it all worked out well and she is very much part of our family. Maureen and I take great pride in the way the three children have turned out and the success they have made of their lives has more than compensated for the tempestuous nature of the background to our own relationship.

I am still involved in football in one form or another. There is some co-commentary work I carry out for Garrison Radio, as the name suggests, covering services football, men and women, most recently matches involving their counterparts in

Germany. It is great fun and the first thing I notice as an ex-professional is the rigid discipline of the players, not a hint of dissent or complaint. I suppose it's too much to expect that automatic military response from the soldiers to the referee as always being right even when he's wrong creeping into the mainstream, but I find it refreshing.

I don't envy referees these days because it is rapidly becoming a non-contact sport with the persistent diving and play-acting, which I believe is having a detrimental effect on the game as a spectacle. My own response to referees was fashioned by my school and as a Middlesbrough apprentice and even if I disagreed with their decisions in the heat of a big match, I could always hear the imaginary voice of George Wardle in my head telling me to shut up and get on with the game.

It would be easy to blame the flood of foreign players in the Premier League and Football League for the injury-feigning but I'm sorry to see home-grown footballers now attempting to emulate the worst habits imported from abroad. You will recall me saying my only two yellow cards came against Newcastle, one for Middlesbrough and one for Southampton five years apart, when the adrenaline was flowing. Being a poor tackler, though never a malicious one, I might have got a few more today where you don't have to do much to get a caution but when I played there was a slightly more robust relationship between officials and players, one where there was greater respect and trust.

Neil Midgley, a prominent referee of my time, even went with us on holiday with his wife Barbara a couple of times but it didn't stop me having a little run-in with him at Brighton during an FA Cup quarter-final. George Lawrence was mouthing off at him and Midgley told me as play continued to shut him up but then a Brighton player kicked the ball away at a free kick and I demanded of him what he was going to do about that. The answer was nothing.

I don't think referees were bothered by me. Keith Hackett was another top official I could always talk to but after one particular game on the artificial pitch at Queens Park Rangers I told the referee concerned he had just produced the worst performance of my life, stern stuff from me, but I have never yet come across an official who was purposely trying to ruin a match. The players do that.

I don't know if it's possible these days to be friends with a referee when you're a player, but it used to be. I hate it when their decisions are minutely examined on television, every error enlarged and speculated upon and every mistake criticised because I don't think it adds anything, only serving to undermine their authority by questioning their judgement and honesty. I never met a referee who was out to make a name for himself at the expense of the match he was supposed to be running. They have a job to do and goal-line technology or any kind of technology might help them do it.

My other link to the game comes through the sportsman's dinners and lunches I put on for charity. It started at Bertie and Sheila's restaurant in Virginia Water, now called Casanova through what was known as the Monday Club and involved him, me, Jean Perrot and poor Bill Laidlaw and has been going now for about 15 years. We have raised money for the RNLI, the Red, White and Blue Appeal into leukaemia research and for Hampshire Football Association's grass roots initiative. A whole string of top football personalities have come along and spoken for me over the years including Keegan, Andy Gray, Jack Charlton, Stiles, Peter Osgood, Duncan McKenzie, Le Tissier, McMenemy, Gordon Strachan, Case, Norman Hunter and Ron Atkinson and I never have any trouble selling tickets to companies and individuals. None of them are paid or have asked for payment.

Barton Storage have been particularly loyal in their support and have been to all my functions and readily contribute.

Three of their number, Keith Bibb, Ian Sinclair and Danny Rodbourne, were rewarded with a trip to talkSPORT to meet Andy Gray, who was a delightful and courteous host.

Only one potential speaker ever let me down and that was Jeff Stelling, the award-winning Sky TV presenter who has a deserved reputation as one of the best in the business. His Saturday afternoon programme is superb television. But every time I have contacted him, and I have done that several times, his secretary has pleaded a full diary and I even confronted him about it at a PFA awards dinner without getting him to change his mind. It prompted me to send him a little letter reminding him of his North-Eastern roots. In it I said not to forget people on the way up because it's a long way down. I ended it by saying, 'I hope your family are well.'

Stelling aside, everyone I have asked to speak has done so willingly and with alacrity and I thank them because over the years we have raised thousands of pounds for those charities.

After-dinner speaking even took me abroad with Alan Ball once in 2006 to the private home of a certain Elwood Forbes at the behest of some friends, Stan and Jean Davies, in Kuwait. They paid for first-class air travel and a top hotel for us both and Alan had around 150 guests spellbound with his many tales and his trademark enthusiastic banter. The football world was much the poorer for his premature passing.

The good news is that those ex-pats in Kuwait would like another visit some time and I know there won't be a shortage of volunteers because fans in all parts of the world love stories about the game they grew up with. Football has such a universal appeal.

14

Life After Football

WHEN I look back on my career and all the players I played with and against I realise how lucky I was to be at my peak in an era of such extravagant talent. This might have worked against me in international terms in that there was fierce competition for England places in every department. I am not sure that is so today, where the depth of international-class ability seems to be remarkably limited for the first time.

I like to think I might have got a few more than three caps if I had been around now and of course I would have been a lot richer. Perhaps, as some people have suggested, I was a little ahead of my time in that many of the systems currently employed in the game would have suited my flexibility, rather than the rigid formations managers sent out in my own career-span. The same used to be said of Martin Peters, who was a great player in 1966 but who would have been much in demand today. I don't think some managers knew how to use me because they couldn't pigeon-hole my virtues. I certainly wasn't a left-winger, I wasn't a striker and I wasn't a defensive midfielder.

Looking back on those players of my time I have come up with a team made up of the best of those I played with and another of those of the best I played against. It was an intriguing journey, sifting through countless footballers before making my selections and there might be a few surprises. In a sort of 4-3-3 formation, right to left, the best 11 I played with were Jim Platt; John Craggs, Stuart Boam, Willie Maddren, Mark Dennis; Bobby Murdoch, Alan Ball, Graeme Souness; Matt Le Tissier, Kevin Keegan and John Hickton.

Apologies to those I have left out, not least Mick Channon, but this I feel is a well-balanced team. Many are self-selecting and I imagine there will be an eyebrow or two raised for instance at my preference for Platt above Peter Shilton but I honestly believe Platt was much underestimated. Shilts had his weaknesses but you can't play 125 times for your country unless you were exceptional and he was. I found Shilton a complex sort of person, a bit of a loner and a law unto himself in many ways. Nobody at Southampton was close to him. But he had this supercilious attitude to his team-mates at times, talking to them as if they were somehow inferior and everyone except him was at fault if a goal went in against him. This was often the way when crosses came into our box. Peter wasn't the best at judging those and relied heavily on big defenders to take the initiative for him, but he was good at allocating blame if it ever went wrong.

We were in Marbella one mid-season when Dennis Rofe and myself called in at a restaurant called Silks to take some presents and souvenirs to some waiters we knew. Shilton, Worthington and Mark Dennis were already there and in front of a packed house of diners, Shilton swore at me at the top of his voice. I won't say what he called me. I am not renowned for picking fights or getting into arguments but I was quite shocked at what he said and where he said it. I went over to him and let him have a piece of my mind in retaliation, albeit more quietly, and in fairness he did later apologise. But Peter was an established world star and the words he chose were unforgivable as was the manner in which he said them. Somehow that was typical of him. Incidentally, a personal grudge, long since resolved, is not the reason I preferred the reliable Platt. I just happen to think he was the better goalkeeper.

The others were all outstanding in their ways, even John Hickton whose selection might seem odd in such illustrious company. I think Keegan would have enjoyed playing alongside him in the way he similarly fed off John Toshack at Liverpool. Hickton was a great player of his type, a big, barnstorming centre-forward who got nowhere near an England cap but who would definitely have been in contention had he been in his prime now. As I said earlier we at Middlesbrough needed to replace him when we got into the First Division because he was just beyond his best and the fact that we never did speaks volumes for his target-man and goalscoring quality and the attributes he brought to the team. John Hickton at his best would always get into my best team.

Picking a team of the best I had played against was just as difficult because there were so many great footballers around at the time and I do mean great. My team, again in a 4-3-3 line-up, is Neville Southall; Tommy Smith, Bobby Moore, Norman Hunter, Kenny Sansom; Terry McDermott, Billy Bremner, Liam Brady; George Best, Kenny Dalglish and Trevor Francis.

Southall was a bit of a shambolic figure off the pitch but between the sticks I never came across his equal. Norman Hunter understudied Moore in the England team and while Hunter may have lacked a little of Moore's class and worldwide repute, they were both very hard to by-pass. Tommy Smith didn't play much for England at all but anyone ever on the receiving end of one of his shuddering tackles knew just how good he was. Kenny Dalglish was supreme in attack and Trevor Francis had this acceleration and skill but above all I'm pleased to be able to select George Best. To a modern generation George will be remembered mostly for his failure to beat alcoholism but my contemporaries, those lucky enough to have seen him in action, will drool for ever over his unique skill. Has Britain ever produced a better pure footballer?

Alcohol was poor old George's undoing and while I was never a big drinker there was plenty of it about in my time. Bryan Robson had a famous thirst and Shilton too but in the main they kept it within bounds and were fit and clear-headed enough to perform when required on a Saturday afternoon.

Thanks to my Italian friend Bertie I have discovered the wonders of red wine and, as my ample figure now testifies, the good food of his home country. Maureen and I have been with them to Florence and to his mother's home, 50 miles to the south-west in Castellina Marittima in Tuscany, to sample the very best of Italian cuisine. In Florence this ranges from lampredotto from a stall outside the indoor market in San Lorenzo, where all the stall-holders love their football, to having lunch or dinner with Bertie's stepmother Mirrella and the Patechi family, Mario, Serena, Ilaria, Valentina and Jacapo in La Casalinga next to Santo Spirito church. Did I say I liked my food?

I can't think of anything better than walking through the streets of Florence, thinking of all the great people who lived and worked there, browsing in the Uffizi Gallery, drifting through the famous Vasari Corridor on the way to all the famous art galleries, palaces and piazzas and stopping for a refreshing fragalino at the Hole-in-the-Wall near Piazza Della Signoria or perhaps an apperativo or espresso at one of the bars in Piazza Della Republica. Not forgetting to rub the pig's nose and drop a coin in the fountain to wish for good luck and to make sure you return to Florence. And we do.

It was in Florence that I witnessed one of the most nasty and vindictive football matches ever. The Calcio Storico Cup it's called and is played for by the four quarters of the city with a semi-final and final in a little arena outside Santa Croce

Church. Bill and Jean Laidlaw were with us and there was a lot of pomp and ceremony beforehand and an unusual number of police and ambulance staff, or so we thought. Each team seemed to have about 20 players and as soon as the whistle went for the start of the match all hell broke loose. It was the most barbaric two minutes of action any of us could remember with fists flying, fighting, kicking, stamping and head-butting as if many old scores were being settled and rivalries renewed.

The match, if I can call it that, was called off almost immediately and those waiting ambulance men were on the pitch in no time. But not the police. Sirens may have been wailing but the police kept their distance as the carnage unfolded in front of them. Only later did we discover that players from all four quarters were mostly criminals who had spent time in prison. Had the police become involved the violence would have got even worse. We waited 20 minutes hoping for a restart but it never happened and we never did find out which quarter, if any, had won the cup.

As to gambling, that other perceived great vice of footballers from my generation, I wouldn't even know how to place a bet – I get Kevin McMahon, the racing expert at the *Southern Daily Echo*, to do that for me – but the big three at Southampton, Keegan, Ball and Channon, lived for their horse racing, as did Terry Cochrane at Middlesbrough. They seemed to know what they were talking about but whether or not they were consistent winners, I very much doubt. I understand the old drinking and gambling culture in professional football is not as prevalent as it used to be and one or two other tricks from the past have gone too, thankfully for the better.

Multi-coloured football boots look a bit strange these days to people like me but they aren't as lethal as some worn by the tough old pros when I started. They used to sit on dressing room benches and pick away at the top layers of the studs so as to expose the nails underneath, all the better for running down the backs of opponents' legs or even across the shins. That's why referees and their assistants still inspect boots, a lingering legacy from the days when defenders took no prisoners and forwards were not protected by strict tackling rules in the way they are now. I am pleased that the old leg-breaking tackles have been properly outlawed but in my time they were part of the game and no one grumbled, although the likes of Channon and Peter Osgood, as two examples, joined me in hobbling into middle age.

Tony Brown was in many ways like me, racking up a huge number of appearances, more than 600 in fact, for West Bromwich and scoring in excess of 200 goals but for England he only got the solitary cap and there might have been many more. But the competition for a forward place in the international team was intense and he will go down, again like me, as a good First Division player who was not fully exposed to the highest level.

I mention Tony for one very good reason. He scored the best goal I ever saw. Tony, a Midlands Footballer of the Year three times, got the goal playing for Albion against Sheffield Wednesday and it's still shown on television today, an overhead half-volley, if you can imagine that, which flew into the net. Bobby Charlton apparently also says Brown's goal was his favourite.

I am often asked which was my favourite ground, and least favourite come to that, and I can honestly say that I was as happy playing at Grantham, as I did, as I was at Old Trafford. The buzz I got was simply from playing football, wherever and whenever. It was all about me expressing myself on any given stage, trying to do better each time, trying to make myself consistent and showing spectators I could play. Wear your jersey with pride was a mantra instilled in us as kids and it remained foremost in my mind to the very end.

I was well paid by the standards of the time and sometimes I would chuckle to myself that I was actually being paid to play football, a game millions across the world play to a greater or lesser extent, mostly for nothing. How lucky was that? My job was to show the fans, the paying customers, who would have loved to be in my position, that I cared and I carried that philosophy with me from England to my coaching stint at Netley Central.

Listening to the National Anthem still fills me with pride. I get very emotional when I hear it at football or rugby matches and at the Olympics and Paralympics. It reminds me of the time I lined up at Wembley in an England shirt, struggling to choke back the tears.

My only hope for the competitors is that they are able to do the best they possibly can and give everything of themselves so that they have no regrets. Not everyone can be a winner, of course, but just taking part in an enormous occasion is an achievement in itself. I suppose that's why I don't like watching England football internationals having experienced them myself. I want the players to do well, I know how good the player must be, I know how much effort they have put in, how hard they've worked just to get there. I know from first-hand experience how much it means to them, I know how dedicated they have to be and how much they want to win. Yet because of how hard the British game is physically and mentally when it comes to the big competitions, usually after gruelling domestic seasons, they find it a step too far every time.

I think we also stifle our natural talent somehow. With players like Steven Gerrard, Frank Lampard, Ashley Cole, Rio Ferdinand, John Terry, Paul Scholes and Wayne Rooney, England should have been winning things. Do they play their natural game? I am not so sure. I fear we have been frightened to express ourselves in major tournaments, too worried about the opposition to try something different individually or as a team. We have always had great players in England and that is still the case, though perhaps, as I have indicated, not so many of them. They need to play with a free spirit within a team set-up. I am convinced it can be done and the world will again see the best of British.

When I played, we were deeply honoured and privileged to be playing for club and country but I'm not sure players feel the same now. Some players give the impression that it is the fans who are privileged, lucky to be watching them play. They have got it the wrong way round, even a disciplinarian like Sir Alex Ferguson does not seem to be able to change that attitude, but the sooner it is changed the better it will be for our game, the game we all love.

Like many ex-players I'm not a good watcher of football. If I'm covering a game for local radio it's acceptable because I can use my professional knowledge to analyse what is happening, to guide the listener through the tactical changes and the formations, leaving the descriptions of the incidents to my co-commentator. But I find it hard to sit down and watch a game as a leisure activity, not least because I find many commentators and pundits have started to believe their own publicity and have become caricatures, and I much prefer watching rugby union and cricket.

Having avoided rugby at school I now find the rule changes have made it much less static and far more open. The sport has developed rapidly in a short time although the sheer size of the participants would make it hard for someone like me ever to have got a game.

Cricket I have always loved. Had Durham been in the County Championship when I was a lad who knows what might have occurred? It doesn't and couldn't happen now but there were a handful of players good enough to play county cricket in the summer and professional football in the winter. The great Denis Compton was a prime example before demanding schedules made that impossible but I played to a decent standard at Durham and I keep an eye on the performances of Durham's county side and my adopted Hampshire. I spent many enthralled hours in the Durham bar and clubhouse listening to the cricket tales of Sam Stoker, vice-master of Hatfield College, and 'Mr Durham City', Ken Allen.

With Peter Hood as the main commentator I have been able to travel up and down England again, re-living my own career and meeting old friends, old team-mates and opponents. We knew all the motorway services, the best and cheapest hotels and where to leave the car without testing my lack of walking mobility.

Peter and I first met at Warwick Services, him picking me out because I had no idea what he looked like, and I remember his astonishment when I ordered my favourite Earl Grey tea. Peter was baffled that any footballer knew what Earl Grey tea was, least of all a lad from Sherburn Road.

I think Peter and I enjoyed getting into the hallowed sanctuary of football club car parks as much as the games themselves at times. I find it hard to walk any great distance so it was up to me to bluff our way in to areas normally reserved only for players and officials and not for the press and public. When Southampton were playing at Ipswich we drove to the car park hoping rather than expecting to get in only to discover the Portman Road car park was full of Sky TV trucks. This called for some sweet-talking and I ordered Peter not to say a word while I dealt with the steward zealously guarding the gate to the inner sanctum.

George Burley and Tony Mowbray were in charge of Ipswich at the time and I told the steward that as an old international friend of theirs they had told me I could park in the main area. Unable to spot my name on his list, the steward was about to tell us to turn around when I played my last gambit, asking him to get on the phone to Burley who would be sure to let us in. Not fancying ringing George over something so trivial, he relented and we were in.

Much the same occurred at Derby, and at Chelsea we got even luckier. I was just going through my routine of ex-England, Southampton etc etc to the car park steward when he interrupted to say, 'You don't have to tell me who you are, David. I watched you many times for Middlesbrough and I'm a great fan. Please accept this pass and go on to the underground car park.'

Peter wasn't the best of drivers, he won't mind me saying, but we toured the country together, took part in the Fair Oak meat draw together and laughed a lot on and off air. With him I saw live football again but since the demise of our radio coverage I don't see any and, yes, I do miss the involvement and the fun. We still meet for a cup or two of Earl Grey tea to reminisce.

The good thing about football is the chance it gives you to meet so many different people in all walks of life and I can't pretend that I haven't used the fact that I am an ex-footballer to obtain an advantage in my business career. One of the perks which came my way was becoming president of Southampton's Isle of Wight Supporters' Club after Nick Holmes had stepped down. The islanders were generous to a fault, especially Ted and Janet Taggart who put so much time and effort into running the club. All the players were invited over there for their annual gathering and paid for us to stay in hotels overnight.

There were others like Ian McFarlane I should have mentioned more often. Ian was another of the hard task-masters Middlesbrough seemed to specialise in; loud, direct but a coach with a great sense of humour. Malcolm Smith, Peter Brine, Peter Creamer, Pat Cuff and Brian Taylor will remember him for the way they were pushed by him in training, making their lives hell when he thought they needed it but he was a big influence on us all during Jack's time. We all enjoyed Jack and his player-incentives and you couldn't help but laugh at some of the tricks he played on us.

Like the time we went to Australia after winning promotion. He promised us each £6 a day spending money until we had boarded the plane when he announced it had been reduced to two. Our five-a-side matches, often involving England against Scotland, had Mars Bars for the winners and a yellow shirt for the player adjudged to have been the worst. Sometimes the prize was a little more interesting than a bar of chocolate. Jack's Manager of the Month award was a gallon of whisky which Stuart Boam cheekily suggested he gave to the players if we beat Notts County in our next match by two clear goals. To our surprise, Jack agreed and we did and, what's more, he duly handed over the whisky.

Jack liked to take forthcoming matches in blocks of five with rewards for a certain number of points. On one occasion we each got a suit, then shirts, club ties and shoes. It turned out Jack knew an accommodating tailor in Leeds.

I was a bit scared of Jack at times. We had just got into the First Division when I felt I should be asking for a pay rise from £20 a week to £25. But I couldn't face him on my own so I got Bill Gates, our PFA rep, to accompany me to his office. I stood there, metaphorically cap-in-hand, as Jack listened to my humble plea put to him by Gates and then quickly agreed to give me what I wanted.

Do I wish I had played for Sunderland? They missed me as a kid and they missed me when I was on my way to Southampton. I drove a car at Middlesbrough sponsored by the Sunderland chairman Tom Cowie and when I handed it back, before the infamous red Mercedes came on the scene, I met Tom at the Gosforth Park Hotel coincidentally and asked why he had not bid for me when it was clear I was available. 'We couldn't afford you,' he told me. 'Not even £600,000.'

I had hoped also, as I said, and even then not seriously, that Lawrie might have taken me with him to Roker Park from Southampton, having brought me south in the first place, but that was a pipe dream of mine, nothing more. So it was not to be. Sunderland are in my blood but of course my main clubs are very definitely Middlesbrough and Southampton and I loved playing for them both.

It was all a far cry from the Sunday night discos at Durham Rugby Club listening to records by my beloved Creedence Clearwater Revival, played for us by Brian Cade, who was best man at my first wedding, with my pals Stevie Foster, Paddy McDee and George Maddox, all of us underage, and a far cry too from Operation Weeting, the police probe into allegations of phone-hacking by *News of the World* journalists.

Little did I ever think I might be involved in something as extraordinary as that, but I was. Gordon Taylor, the PFA chief executive, was awarded £700,000 compensation after his mobile had been hacked into by the private investigator Glenn Mulcaire. Later it was found that my number had been downloaded by Mulcaire on to his laptop following calls I had made to Taylor and at the time of writing I'm waiting to see if there might be further developments.

I owe a lot to Gordon and the PFA for the way they helped me through some very difficult times with my injury and when I was out of work and to the Middlesbrough Ex-Players' Association, in particular to Jim Platt, Gordon Jones and Alan Peacock for the same reason. They were dark times when I needed help and support and I got both from those organisations.

Maureen and I will always be grateful to them as we are to our friends Stan and Jean Davies, Jean and Beverley Perrot, Lyn Carpenter, Karen Heath and Warren Aspinall, Maureen Capel, Michele and Trevor Meller and Doug and Brenda Taylor, all of whom understood our problems and offered us physical and moral support at our lowest points. Without them and Maureen's sympathetic sisters, Kathleen and her husband Alan, Sheila and her late husband David, her brother John and wife Maureen, and her late brother Terry, I'm not sure what would have been the outcome.

I can't forget, either, when my divorce was causing so many ructions and difficulties the support I received from my family; from my brothers and sisters, Billy, John, Joseph, Jeanette and Susan and their respective spouses Winnie, Stella, Peter and Tommy and John's widow, Pat. They were there for me when I needed them most.

I have met people through football I would never have otherwise met and for that I must be grateful. One of them was the comedian Freddie Starr who left an indelible mark on those of us at Middlesbrough who remember him training with us while he was in panto nearby. Freddie was the same with us as when he was appearing on stage, larger than life. One day he jumped in the communal bath after training with the rest of us and then got out again. No one thought anything of it until, to our horror, we saw he had left a deposit floating in the water. You have never seen a group of men vacate a bath as quickly.

More seriously, Kevin Keegan has been kind enough to say a few words as a foreword to this book and he says I did what was 'written on the tin', which I take as a great compliment. Kevin was also surprised I had played so little for England. Maybe my consistency counted against me and I think I paid the price for not being more flamboyant. He was right also that there was plenty of quality competition for the positions in the England team I might have occupied but in the end Bobby Robson chose not to pick me when I was in my prime and there was nothing much I could have done about that.

It is true also that Middlesbrough and Southampton are not the most fashionable of clubs but I have no regrets whatever in having devoted my career to them. I have nothing but the fondest of memories of them both, the players, the officials, the fans' and I made friends in football and outside it who will be friends forever.

If my story warns of anything it's that more could be done to help footballers when they finish the game or when the game finishes with them. For those lucky enough to play into their 30s there are still another 30 or more working years left and, for all the money now awash in football, only a minority retire rich enough never to need worry about the mortgage again. For the vast majority, even people like me who played for so long at the top level, there is this huge void, the uncertainty, the fear. In my case I was limping painfully to the dole office four years after representing my country and there is plenty of evidence to indicate I was not alone among footballers in hitting rock-bottom. There are examples of depression and suicides.

I had ample time to consider my plight as I lay on that couch watching the woodpecker, the blissful memories of my footballing career small compensation for what I was then having to endure. Luckily, through it all, I had Maureen and my family to see me through the worst times and to keep thinking positively.

As I write these last few words I'm recovering from a broken right ankle as the result of a fall down the stairs at home. I am also counting the cost of driving my car into the back of another, but those sort of things happen to everyone.

When I was a little lad growing up on Sherburn Road I never imagined the sort of life I've had. I wanted to be a footballer and that's what I became. To that extent I fulfilled my dreams and those of my contemporaries who were not as gifted in that respect as me. I hope my story will show a few people that not all footballers live privileged existences and there is a downside to fame. But I am happy now; the worst, I hope, is over for ever. Instead I can look back on some glorious times and remember that, one way or another, I have been extremely lucky.

David Armstrong's Career Statistics
Birthplace: Durham
Date of birth: 26 December 1954

	League		League Cup		FA Cup		UEFA Cup	
	A	G	A	G	A	G	A	G
Middlesbrough								
1971/72	5+1	0	0	0	0	0	0	0
1972/73	19+1	1	1+1	0	0	0	0	0
1973/74	42	5	3	0	2	1	0	0
1974/75	42	5	5	1	6	1	0	0
1975/76	42	6	6	1	2	0	0	0
1976/77	42	8	1	0	5	4	0	0
1977/78	42	6	4	2	5	1	0	0
1978/79	42	11	2	0	2	0	0	0
1979/80	42	11	3	2	3	1	0	0
1980/81	39	6	2	0	4	0	0	0
Southampton								
1981/82	41	15	1	0	1	0	3	1
1982/83	41	8	5	1	1	0	2	0
1983/84	42	15	3	2	6	2	0	0
1984/85	35	10	4	0	3	0	1	0
1985/86	41	10	6	3	6	2	0	0
1986/87	22	1	4	0	0	0	0	0
AFC Bournemouth								
1987/88	6+3	2	2	1	0	0	0	0
TOTAL	585+5	120	52+1	13	46	12	6	1

Summary

Middlesbrough								
	357+2	59	27+1	6	29	8	0	0
Southampton								
	222	59	23	6	17	4	6	1
AFC Bournemouth								
	6+3	2	2	1	0	0	0	0

Notes: The appearances column denotes full appearances + appearances as substitute.

Goals

100th league goal: For Southampton v Newcastle United at The Dell on 24 November 1984.

First league goal for Middlesbrough: v Aston Villa at Villa Park on 28 October 1972.

Last league goal for Middlesbrough: v Arsenal at Highbury on 28 February 1981.

First league goal for Southampton: v West Ham United at Upton Park on 22 September 1981.

Last league goal for Southampton: v Liverpool at The Dell on 20 September 1986.

First league goal for AFC Bournemouth: v Bradford City at Dean Court on 22 August 1987.

Last league goal for AFC Bournemouth: v Birmingham City at St Andrew's on 29 August 1987.

Club Honours

Second Division champions 1973/74 with Middlesbrough.

Anglo-Scottish Cup winners 1975/76 with Middlesbrough.

Middlesbrough Player of the Year 1979/80.

First Division runners-up 1983/84 with Southampton.

Southampton Player of the Year 1983/84.

Career Milestones

100th league appearance: For Middlesbrough v Stoke City at Ayresome Park on 1 March 1975.

200th league appearance: For Middlesbrough v Coventry City at Highfield Road on 17 September 1977.

300th league appearance: For Middlesbrough v Crystal Palace at Selhurst Park on 29 December 1979.

400th league appearance: For Southampton v Arsenal at Highbury on 15 May 1982.

500th league appearance: For Southampton v Norwich City at Carrow Road on 12 January 1985.

First and Last League Appearances

Middlesbrough: Debut v Blackpool at Bloomfield Road on 3 April 1972; last appearance v Liverpool at Ayresome Park on 5 May 1981.

Southampton: Debut v Wolverhampton Wanderers at The
Dell on 1 September 1981; last appearance v Coventry
City at Highfield Road on 9 May 1987.
AFC Bournemouth: Debut v Sheffield United at Bramall Lane
on 15 August 1987; last appearance v Barnsley at Oakwell
on 8 March 1988.

Consecutive Appearances
305 league appearances for Middlesbrough from 24 March
1973 to 30 August 1980.
356 appearances in all competitions (including Football
League, League Cup and FA Cup) for Middlesbrough from
24 March 1973 to 2 September 1980.
Both of the above are Middlesbrough club records for
consecutive appearances.

Miscellaneous
A total of 87 per cent of the league games which David
appeared in were in Division One (equivalent to today's
Premier League) with the remaining 13 per cent of matches
played in the Second Division (equivalent to today's
Championship).
David played in 93 per cent of Middlesbrough's league games
from April 1972 to May 1981.
David played in 88 per cent of Southampton's league games
during his stay at the club.
David's career total of 146 goals in all competitions was
scored against 50 different clubs.
The opponents he scored the most goals against were
Arsenal; 12 in all competitions (ten league, one League
Cup and one FA Cup). He scored six against Arsenal while
playing for Middlesbrough and six with Southampton. A
further coincidence is that this was also the most goals he
scored against an opponent for his respective clubs.
David made five league appearances for Middlesbrough
against his future employees, Southampton, and scored one
goal but finished on the winning side only once with the
other games ending in a draw and three defeats.

He played against Middlesbrough on three occasions for
Southampton, with the Saints winning all three games (two
League and one FA Cup).

INTERNATIONAL HONOURS

England Under-23
Appearances: 4
Goals: 0

v Portugal Under-23 at Lisbon (European Under-23
Championship) on 19 November 1974.
v Wales Under-23 at Wrexham (friendly) on 21 January 1975.
v Czechoslovakia Under-23 at Trnava (European Under-23
Championship) on 28 October 1975.
v Portugal Under-23 at Selhurst Park (European Under-23
Championship) on 18 November 1975.

England B
Appearances: 2
Goals: 0

v Spain B at Roker Park (friendly) on 26 March 1980.
v USA at Old Trafford (friendly) on 14 October 1980.

Full internationals
Appearances: 3
Goals: 0

v Australia at Sydney Cricket Ground (friendly) on 31 May
1980.
v West Germany at Wembley (friendly) on 13 October 1982.
v Wales at Wrexham (British International Championship) on
2 May 1984.